AQA Religious Studies A

Judaism

GCSE

Anne Jordan

Steven Mintz

Peter Smith

Series editor

Cynthia Bartlett

Nelson Thornes

Published in 2009 by:

Nelson Thornes Ltd
Delta Place
27 Bath Road
CHELTENHAM
GL53 7TH
United Kingdom

09 10 11 12 13 / 10 9 8 7 6 5 4 3 2 1

A catalogue record for this book is available from the British Library

ISBN 978 1 4085 0478 9

Cover photograph: Getty/Stockbyte
Page make-up by Pantek Arts Ltd, Maidstone
Printed and bound in Spain by GraphyCems

Acknowledgements
The author and publisher are grateful to the following for permissions to the reproduce photographs and other copyright material:

Text acknowledgements
Scripture quotations taken from the Holy Bible, New International Version. Copyright © 1978, 1984 by International Bible Society. Used by permission of Hodder & Stoughton, a division of Hodder Headline Ltd. All rights reserved. 'NIV' is a registered trademark of International Bible Society. UK trademark number 1448790.
2.3: Extract from *Belsen in History and Memory* edited by Joanne Reilly et al. Copyright © Reprinted with permission.
4.1: Extract from Guide to Judaism www.somethingjewish.co.uk © Reproduced with permission.
4.2: Extract from farm animals department, RSPCA website 'What is the RSPCA's view of religious slaughter?' Copyright © Reproduced with permission.
6.5: Extract from www.guardian.co.uk/world/2009/feb/08/police-patrols-antisemitism-jewish-community. Copyright © Guardian News & Media Ltd, 2009; Reproduced with permission.
Extract from www.jcore.org.uk/whatwedo.php. Copyright © Jewish Council for Racial Equality; Reproduced with permission.
6.10: Extract from Anne Frank *Diary of a Young Girl* Copyright © Penguin; Reprinted with permission.

Photo acknowledgements
Alamy 1.10B, 2.6B, 2.7B, 3.3B, 3.7B, 3.10A, 3.10B, 5.7B, 6.2B, 6.2C, 6.7B **Ark Religion** 4.2B, 4.4B, 4.9B, 5.9B **Art Directors** 3.4B **Corbis** 2.3A, 2.7A, 3.3B, 4.1B **Getty** 2.4B, 3.3C **Fotolia** 1.1A, 1.1B, 1.2A, 1.2C, 1.3A, 1.4A, 1.4B, 1.5A, 1.6B, 1.7A, 1.8A, 1.10A, 1.11A, 2.1A, 2.2A, 3.1B, 3.3A, 3.7A, 3.8, 3.9A, 3.9B, 4.1A, 4.2C, 4.4A, 4.5A, 4.5C, 4.5D, 4.6A, 4.6B, 4.6D, 5.1B, 5.3A, 5.6B, 5.8B, 6.3B, 6.4, 6.5A, 6.7A **Istock** 1.3B, 1.5B, 1.5C, 1.7B, 1.9B, 2.1B, 2.3B, 2.4A, 2.5A, 2.5B, 2.5C, 2.6A, 2.8A, 2.8B, 2.9A, 2.9B, 2.9C, 2.10A, 2.10B, 2.11A, 3.1A, 3.2A, 3.2B, 3.2D, 3.4A, 3.4, 3.5A, 3.5B, 3.6B, 4.1C, 4.3A, 4.3B, 4.3C, 4.4B, 4.4C, 4.5B, 4.7A, 4.7B, 4.8A, 4.8B, 4.8C, 4.9B, 4.10A, 4.10B, 5.1A, 5.4A, 5.4B, 5.5A, 5.6A, 5.7A, 5.9A, 5.10A, 6.1B, 6.3A, 6.6A, 6.8A **Jcore** 6.5C, 6.5D **Press Association** 1.9A, 2.2B, 6.6B, 6.8B **Peter Smith** 5.2A, 6.9a, 6.10 **Rex** 1.6A

Contents

Nelson Thornes has worked in partnership with AQA to make sure that this book offers you the best possible support for your GCSE course. All the content has been approved by the senior examining team at AQA, so you can be sure that it gives you just what you need when you are preparing for your exams.

How to use this book

This book covers everything you need for your course.

Learning Objectives

At the beginning of each section or topic you'll find a list of Learning Objectives based on the requirements of the specification, so you can make sure you are covering everything you need to know for the exam.

Objectives

Objectives

Objectives

Objectives

First objective.

Second objective.

AQA Examiner's Tips

Don't forget to look at the AQA Examiner's Tips throughout the book to help you with your study and prepare for your exam.

AQA   Examiner's tip

Don't forget to look at the AQA Examiner's Tips throughout the book to help you with your study and prepare for your exam.

AQA Examination-style Questions

These offer opportunities to practise doing questions in the style that you can expect in your exam so that you can be fully prepared on the day.

AQA examination questions are reproduced by permission of the Assessment and Qualifications Alliance.

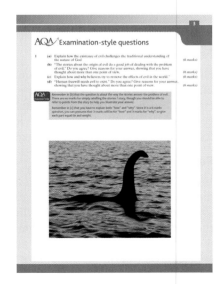

AQA GCSE Judaism

This book is written specifically for GCSE students studying the AQA Religious Studies Specification A, *Unit 11 Judaism*. You will be studying six very different aspects of Jewish beliefs, teachings, practices and lifestyle. Many of the beliefs and teachings are from the Tenakh (the Jewish Scriptures) as it is the main written authority in Judaism. It has also had a great influence on Jewish practices and lifestyle. You do not have to be Jewish to be successful in this course but an interest in Religious Studies and in Judaism combined with a willingness to find out more will help you.

■ Topics in this unit

In the examination, you will be asked to answer questions based on the following six topics.

Beliefs and sources of authority

This first topic underpins much of the rest of this book because understanding the beliefs and sources of authority of Jews will help you to understand their attitudes, lifestyles and practices. Here you will learn about the written sources of authority, concepts of God and the Covenant established between God and the Jewish people.

The synagogue and worship

This topic will help you to understand how places of worship reflect and affect the style of worship that takes place within them. You will study leadership of worship, features within a synagogue and the prayers that are offered there.

Festivals and pilgrimage

Here you will learn in depth about the origins and observance of four festivals – Shabbat, Rosh Hashanah, Yom Kippur and Pesach. You will also consider the place of pilgrimage in the Jewish faith, focusing on two sites in Jerusalem.

Personal lifestyle

In this topic you will learn about Jewish views on dietary laws, i.e. what they can and cannot eat, together with laws that govern the special clothes they wear in worship and for some Orthodox Jews in their everyday lives. You will also look at the special laws that make Shabbat a special day.

Family life

Ceremonies to celebrate birth, coming of age and marriage will be considered along with the commemoration of death. In addition, the importance of the family unit will be considered along with the wider Jewish community based on the synagogue.

Justice and equality

The final topic explores Jewish views on prejudice and discrimination, the role and status of women and suffering. There is a strong focus on persecution based on prejudice and discrimination which was seen most strongly in the Holocaust.

■ Assessment guidance

Your examination will be in two parts. Part A will have four questions split into shorter parts. You have to answer all of the questions in part A, which will total 48 marks.

Part B will contain two questions. Again, they will be split into smaller parts. You are required to answer just one of these questions. Each of these questions carries 24 marks so they are longer than in part A and it is likely that you will have to give more detail in some of your answers.

Every chapter in this book finishes with assessment guidance, using questions similar in style to those in your examination. There is also a summary of what you have learnt in the topic together with a sample answer to one part for you to mark yourself. The large grid opposite will help you to do this as well as finding out what you have to do to gain high marks.

Examination questions will test two assessment objectives

AO1	Describe, explain and analyse, using knowledge and understanding.	50%
AO2	Use evidence and reasoned argument to express and evaluate personal responses, informed insights and differing viewpoints.	50%

The examiner will also take into account the quality of your written communication – how clearly you express yourself and how well you communicate your meaning. The grid below also gives you some guidance on the sort of quality examiners expect to see at different levels.

Levels of response mark scheme

Levels	Criteria for AO1	Criteria for AO2	Quality of written communication	Marks
0	Nothing relevant or worthy of credit	An unsupported opinion or no relevant evaluation	The candidate's presentation, spelling, punctuation and grammar seriously obstruct understanding	0 marks
Level 1	Something relevant or worthy of credit	An opinion supported by simple reason	The candidate presents some relevant information in a simple form. The text produced is usually legible. Spelling, punctuation and grammar allow meaning to be derived, although errors are sometimes obstructive	1 mark
Level 2	Elementary knowledge and understanding, e.g. two simple points	An opinion supported by one developed reason or two simple reasons		2 marks
Level 3	Sound knowledge and understanding	An opinion supported by one well developed reason or several simple reasons. **N.B. Candidates who make no religious comment should not achieve more than Level 3**	The candidate presents relevant information in a way which assists with the communication of meaning. The text produced is legible. Spelling, punctuation and grammar are sufficiently accurate not to obscure meaning	3 marks
Level 4	A clear knowledge and understanding with some development	An opinion supported by two developed reasons with reference to religion		4 marks
Level 5	A detailed answer with some analysis, as appropriate	Evidence of reasoned consideration of two different points of view, showing informed insights and knowledge and understanding of religion	The candidate presents relevant information coherently, employing structure and style to render meaning clear. The text produced is legible. Spelling, punctuation and grammar are sufficiently accurate to render meaning clear	5 marks
Level 6	A full and coherent answer showing good analysis, as appropriate	A well-argued response, with evidence of reasoned consideration of two different points of view showing informed insights and ability to apply knowledge and understanding of religion effectively		6 marks

Note: In evaluation answers to questions worth only 3 marks, the first three levels apply. Questions which are marked out of 3 marks do not ask for two views, but reasons for your own opinion.

Successful study of this unit will result in a Short Course GCSE award. Study of one further unit will provide a Full Course GCSE award. Other units in Specification A which may be taken to achieve a Full Course GCSE award are:

- Unit 1 Christianity
- Unit 2 Christianity: Ethics
- Unit 3 Roman Catholicism
- Unit 4 Roman Catholicism: Ethics
- Unit 5 St Mark's Gospel
- Unit 6 St Luke's Gospel
- Unit 7 Philosophy of Religion
- Unit 8 Islam
- Unit 9 Islam: Ethics
- Unit 11 Judaism: Ethics
- Unit 12 Buddhism
- Unit 13 Hinduism
- Unit 14 Sikhism

1.1 Tenakh

The **Tenakh** is the holy book used in Judaism. The name Tenakh is formed from the first letters of each of the three divisions of the Tenakh: *Torah* – the Five Books of Moses; *Nevi'im* – Prophets; and *Ketuvim* – Writings. These three words are combined together to form the word **TeNaKh**. The books of the Tenakh are also included in Christian Bibles. Christians often refer to the Tenakh as the Old Testament.

Jews believe that much of the contents of the Tenakh were compiled by a group of scholars and leaders known as 'Men of the Great Assembly' (in Hebrew 'Anshei Knesset Hagedolah'). The task of compiling the Tenakh was finished by 450 BCE, since when it has remained unchanged.

Contents of the Tenakh

Torah

The **Torah** (meaning 'teaching') consists of the first five books of the Tenakh. It is often referred to as the 'Five Books of Moses'. The Torah is the most sacred object in Judaism and is a handwritten parchment scroll that is kept in a special cupboard or ark in a place of honour in synagogues. When the Torah is printed it is commonly referred to as a 'Chumash'.

Nevi'im

Nevi'im literally translated means 'prophets'. This section of the Tenakh consists of eight books, starting with the book of Joshua. The Nevi'im are often subdivided into the Earlier Prophets, which are mainly historical, and the Latter Prophets, which are more prophetic.

Ketuvim

Ketuvim means 'writings' or 'scriptures' and consists of 11 books. These books include all the remaining books of the Tenakh including the five Megillot or 'scrolls' that are read as part of the celebrations and observance of festival and fast days during the Jewish calendar year.

Objectives

- Examine the structure and contents of the Tenakh.
- Examine the role of the Tenakh in the everyday lives of Jews.
- Examine how different denominations in Judaism view the authority of the Tenakh.

Key terms

Tenakh: the 24 books of the Jewish scriptures.

Torah: the five books of Moses and first section of the Tenakh – the law.

Nevi'im: the second section of the Tenakh – the prophets.

Ketuvim: the third section of the Tenakh – the writings.

A A page from a Hebrew Tenakh

B A Torah scroll

The Tenakh

The Torah   The Prophets (Nevi'im)   The Writings (Ketuvim)

GENESIS EXODUS LEVITICUS NUMBERS DEUTERONOMY | JOSHUA JUDGES SAMUEL KINGS | ISAIAH JEREMIAH EZEKIEL | HOSEA JOEL AMOS OBADIAH JONAH MICAH NAHUM HABAKKUK ZEPHANIAH HAGGAI ZECHARIAH MALACHI | PSALMS PROVERBS JOB SONG OF SONGS RUTH LAMENTATIONS ECCLESIASTES ESTHER DANIEL EZRA & NEHEMIAH CHRONICLES

The Books of the Law

The Former Prophets

The Latter (or 'major' Prophets)

The 'minor' Prophets, collected together in one book

Wisdom books

'The Five Scrolls'

Book of Prophesy

Books of History

C Structure of the Tenakh

D Reading the five Megillot

Which Scroll is read?	What day is it read on?
Book of Esther	Purim
Song of Songs	Passover
Book of Ruth	Pentecost or Shavuoth
Lamentations	The Fast of the 9th of Av
Ecclesiastes	Tabernacles or Succoth

The Ketuvim section of the Tenakh is organised as follows:

- five Scrolls: *Esther, Song of Songs*, *Ruth, Lamentations, Ecclesiastes*
- Wisdom Books: *Proverbs, Job, Psalms*
- *Ezra, Nehemiah* and *Chronicles, Daniel*.

The authority of the Tenakh

- Orthodox Jews regard the Torah as the word of God revealed to the people of Israel at Mount Sinai in approximately 1280 BCE.
- The Tenakh is the development of the religious ideas of the Torah as pronounced by the Prophets and through the later writings.
- The word of the Torah is considered divine and timeless and therefore cannot be altered.
- Progressive Jews (sometimes referred to as 'Reform Jews') hold the view that the Torah was written by a person or persons inspired by God. As such, Reform Jews believe that God's will was revealed to human beings gradually and therefore the laws developed over a period of time.
- These different viewpoints have resulted in basic differences in belief between Orthodox and Progressive Jews, which have resulted in a degree of separation in worship and religious practice.

AQA Examiner's tip

You should be able to name the divisions of the Tenakh, in English or in Hebrew, and know something of its significance in the lives of Jews today.

links

For more information on types of worship in Judaism see 2.1 on pages 30–31.

Activities

2 Explain the differences between the Torah, Nevi'im and Ketuvim.

3 How do Reform Jews differ from Orthodox Jews in their beliefs about the authority of the Tenakh?

Summary

You should now have an understanding of the structure of the Tenakh, and the role it plays in the lives of Jews, as well as differences between denominations.

1.2 Talmud

Traditional Jewish belief holds that the Torah revealed to the nation of Israel at Mount Sinai was recorded in its pure form as the Written Law.

At the same time that the Written Law was given to the people, Moses received the detailed teachings of the way in which the Torah should be interpreted. This teaching was oral and became known as the Oral Law.

> 66 *Moses received the Torah at Sinai and handed it to Joshua, Joshua to the elders, the elders to the prophets, and the prophets to the men of the Great Assembly.* 99
>
> *Ethics of the Fathers Authorised Daily Prayer Book*

As the Oral Law was transmitted from generation to generation, there was, of course, a danger of details being altered or misinterpreted, and in 200 CE, the law was collated and written down as the **Mishnah** by Rabbi Judah Hanassi. The Mishnah was arranged in six orders, or parts/sections, each one known in Hebrew as a 'Seder'. Each Seder deals with a different general aspect of the Oral Law.

In 500 CE the writings that summarised the discussion and debate about the Mishnah were collected and organised and became known as the **Gemara**. The combination of the Mishnah and Gemara is known as the **Talmud**. There are two versions of the Talmud.

The actual process of debating the Mishnah and therefore writing the Gemara took place in two separate centres: the Land of Israel and Babylon. The older of the two works is called the Jerusalem Talmud and was compiled during the 4th century CE, while the Babylonian Talmud was not completed until 500 CE.

The Talmud is studied extensively in colleges of advanced Jewish Studies known as Yeshivot.

The six orders of the Talmud

The six sections of the Talmud are given different names, connected with their content.

The Talmud in modern Jewish life

The Talmud is regarded as the central feature of Orthodox Jewish life, and all Jews are encouraged to study it extensively as part of their Jewish education. Regular lectures and extended lessons are held in every major Jewish community. There is a worldwide study circle that offers daily study of the Talmud in a structure that allows Jews to study the same portion of the Talmud wherever they are in the world.

The Talmud is regarded as the source for all Jewish legal teachings and decisions that affect every aspect of a Jew's life. The Talmud is written in the ancient language known as Aramaic, the language spoken by Jews in Israel in the 1st century BCE and 1st century CE.

Objectives

Examine the development and basic structure of the Talmud.

Examine the role of the Talmud in the everyday lives of Jews.

Evaluate the importance of the Talmud for Jews today.

Key terms

Mishnah: the first written version of the oral tradition; the authoritative document was put together in 200 CE.

Gemara: a commentary on the Mishnah, which is part of the Talmud.

Talmud: a commentary by the rabbis on the Torah – Mishnah and Gemara together in one collection.

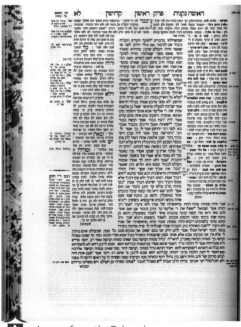

A *A page from the Talmud*

∞ links

The term Yeshivah (plural Yeshivot) is defined in 1.3 on page 12.

B   *The six sections of the Talmud*

Order	Content
Seeds (Zeraim)	Prayer, blessings, tithes and agricultural laws
Festival (Moed)	Laws of Shabbat and Festivals
Women (Nashim)	Marriage, divorce, some forms of oaths and the laws of the Nazirite
Damages (Nezikin)	Both civil and criminal law, the running of the courts and oaths
Holy things (Kodashim)	Sacrificial rites, and the dietary laws, and the Temple
Purities (Tohorot)	Laws of purity and impurity, including the impurity of the dead, the laws of ritual purity for the priests and the laws of 'family purity'

C   *The Talmud is studied extensively in Yeshivot*

Activities

1   Choose one of the orders of the Talmud and try to write down as many different topics that you think might be covered by it.

2   Why is Talmud study not regarded as important by some Jews?

Research activity

Daf Yomi is a popular system of Talmud study. Use the internet to research and learn more about it.

Some Jews do not regard the Talmud as being so important, however, and tend not to study it. Some also find that Aramaic is too difficult to understand and they feel that the Talmud is therefore not easy to access. Many feel that the debates contained in the Talmud, which were written in the 6th century, are not relevant today. People have produced modern English versions of the Talmud, which more Jews can read and these have become very popular.

Extension activity

Read the Talmudic story in the case study. Write your own interpretation of this story in which you explain how Rabbi Akiva found motivation to study.

Rabbi Akiva (50–135CE)

Rabbi Akiva became a Talmudic scholar late on in life. He began as a humble shepherd, but was encouraged to study by his wife who saw his potential. Akiva found this difficult until one day he was sitting by the side of a stream, and was watching with fascination as water constantly dripped onto a stone. He noticed how the action of the water had worn away the rock. This motivated Akiva to study for 40 years and he eventually became the leading scholar of his generation. He is considered to be one of the founders of the Rabbinic School of Jewish commentary.

Case study

Summary

You should now know the basic structure of the Talmud, and understand its role and importance in the lives of Jews today.

What does the word Halakhah mean?

The Torah lists and describes the 613 commandments (mitzvot), but significantly does not expand on the detailed way in which to keep them *in practice*. According to Jewish tradition, when God gave Moses the details of the mitzvot, he also transmitted the details of how to keep them. This detail is described as **Halakhah**. The word Halakhah can be best translated as 'going', as the idea of Halakhah is that by observing the commandments, Jews are 'going with God'. The details of the Halakhah are contained in the Oral Torah.

Responsa

The Talmud is a large and complex work. Rabbis needed a very full knowledge of the entire Talmud, so that they could find the correct reference point, in order to be able to answer questions about Halakhah.

It was also very important for rabbis to be up to date with the latest decisions about matters of Halakhah that other rabbis had made. In order to achieve this they developed a system known as **Responsa**.

A group of learned rabbis and experts on Halakhah were identified in the 7th century. These men held important and responsible positions within the Jewish world. Members of this group used to receive detailed questions from rabbis around the world and would send replies (Responsa).

Eventually, these responses were collected and published so that rabbis and teachers could use them for explaining the solutions to problems about Halakhah.

Halakhah as part of an ongoing process

The world is constantly changing, and the way that we live and observe the world is changing too. It is necessary for Halakhah to be able to match the demands of change; Jews believe that following Halakhah is a way of demonstrating their loyalty to God.

The following extract from the Babylonian Talmud demonstrates how Halakhah evolved as a result of discussion and in some cases conflicting views – in this case a disagreement between the great Talmudic schools of Hillel and his colleague and contemporary Shammai:

> 66 *In debating the order of the lighting of Chanukah candles, Shammai rules that we should light 8 candles on the first night, 7 on the second, 6 on the third and so on until we light but 1 candle on the last night. Hillel disagrees saying that we should light 1 on the first night and then should increase by one extra candle every night until we light 8 candles on the last night.* 99
>
> *Babylonian Talmud*

Developments in modern living and in science and technology have resulted in questions that would not have been considered in the past.

Objectives

Examine the meaning and application of Halakhah.

Examine the role of the Bet Din and Yeshivah in the application of Halakah.

Key terms

Halakhah: the code of conduct for Jewish life.

Responsa: the correspondence of rabbis concerning religious decisions.

Bet Din: religious court, made up of rabbis.

Yeshivah (plural Yeshivot): a college where the Torah and Talmud are studied.

A   *Advances in technology can lead to questions that haven't been considered before*

Research activities

1 Which ruling became accepted by Jews?

2 What was Shammai's reason for his ruling, and what was Hillel's reason for his?

The use of technology in Halakhah is now a complex and fascinating area – the issues of medical ethics or how computers may be used to help in Sabbath observance for example.

A good example of the use of technology for Sabbath observance is the use of time switches to operate heating and lighting in the home without desecrating the Sabbath.

In order to be able to support the work of rabbis as they attempt to provide decisions that respond to the demands of modern situations, many specialised works of Halakhah are constantly being published. The production of these works is continual and ongoing.

Bet Din

Bet Din is the term used to describe a Jewish Rabbinic Court. The name Bet Din is best translated as 'House of Law' and every sizeable Jewish community will have a Bet Din.

Highly qualified rabbis who are specialists in Halakhah sit as members of the Bet Din and are often given the title of 'judges' (dayanim). The role of the Bet Din is vital within the community as it helps organise all Halakhic issues that affect the community. These range from questions regarding kosher food to authorising marriages and holding divorce courts in order to dissolve marriages that have failed.

A Bet Din can act in a case in which two Jews are having a dispute about something and need the matter settled. When a Bet Din offers a legal ruling within Halakhah, then this is binding on the two parties within the dispute.

Yeshivah

Halakhah is a complex subject, and years of study are involved for those who wish to have an excellent knowledge and understanding. Specialist colleges or schools of advanced study of the Talmud and the Halakhah are known as **yeshivot** (singular: **yeshivah**).

Orthodox Jews regard a period of time spent in study at a yeshivah as an important part of their son's education, and take great care over the choice of which yeshivah to send them to. Boys are normally expected to attend a yeshivah at the age of 16. The Talmud forms the basis of the curriculum.

The style of study is quite unique, as it is done on a paired learning system – two students will learn together in a style that resembles a debate, with each contributing to the learning process.

The subjects learned at a yeshivah are an important part of the ongoing relationship that Jews have with God, as well as providing essential Jewish continuity making sure Jews have a good understanding of their faith.

Activities

1. Why do Jews believe that a Yeshivah education is important?
2. Design a poster advertising the opening of a new Yeshivah in your town. Try to make the poster as informative as possible.
3. 'There is no point in Yeshivah study. Boys should get a modern education.' Do you agree? Give reasons to support your answer and show more than one point of view.

∞ links

Read more about the Covenant in 1.7 on pages 20–21.

B A Yeshivah

∞ links

Read more about the work of the Bet Din in Chapter 4, pages 90–91.

AQA Examiner's tip

You should be able to understand the relationship between the Torah and the development of Halakhah as an ongoing process.

Extension activity

Discuss the view that Halakhah interferes too much in the life of a Jew today.

Summary

You should now understand the meaning and application of Halakhah, and how it is applied through the Bet Din and the yeshivah.

שלה ת מיי ף : מס'
ממרים בלגם •
מוש"ע י"ד סילם סע"ג: דלא מפקידנא ועבדינא • מכאן
מדקדק ר"ה לנסים מברכום
על מלוח עשה שהזמן גרמא אנ"ג
דפטורות לגמרי דאפילו מדרבנן לא ... שיהלך ארבע אמות בקומה זקופה שנא'
ו'מלא כל הארץ כבודו רב הונא בריה דרב
יהושע ילא מסני ארבע אמות בגילוי הראש
אמר שכינה למעלה מראשי שאל בן אלמנה ... לנשוח אמר לי אבא ואימא הטיב
בלשון שחוק : מורו וסורו למאמרום
סרפעוגוס • כ"ש שמיב אדם כבכודו
שאף הוא שותף בבריאתו כאביו ואמו

1.4   The concept of God

The Shema

> ❝ Hear, O Israel, the Lord our God, the Lord is One. ❞
>
> *Deuteronomy 6:4*

Objectives

Examine the Shema and the unity of God.

Key terms

Shema: Jewish prayer affirming belief in the one God, found in the Torah.

This sentence is the opening line of the **Shema**, which is one of the most important prayers in Judaism. It is recited twice a day as part of the morning and evening service. The importance of this prayer lies in the belief that it declares the most basic principle in Judaism – the belief in one God. This is most commonly described as monotheism (mono = one; theos = god).

Historically, monotheism was the way that Jews separated themselves from their neighbours who believed in a variety of gods, each of which controlled a different aspect of their lives. This belief is known as polytheism (poly = many).

From this belief in one God, Jews developed the idea that this belief affected the way they lived their lives. So this one supreme God was not only responsible for creating the world and everything that is in it, but was also the source of all morality and values, affecting decisions about life and behaviour.

A   The Shema

In this way we can see that monotheism is more than just a belief. It is really best described as a way of viewing the world and all its contents. By viewing the world in this way, Jews regard every aspect of their lives, both physical and spiritual, as being controlled by God. Everything that a person sees, hears and experiences is regarded by Jews as being a meeting with God, and is best summarised in the belief that is contained in the opening statement of the Shema, that 'God is One'. The religious expression for this belief is to accept 'the Unity of God'.

The first paragraph of the Shema contains many important teachings about God.

Beliefs and teachings

Hear, O Israel, the Lord our God the Lord is One.

Love the Lord (Hashem) your God with **all your heart** and with **all your soul** and with **all your strength**. These Commandments that I give you today are to be upon your hearts. **Impress them on your children**. Talk about them when you walk along the road, when you lie down and when you get up. Tie them as symbols on your hands and bind them on your foreheads. Write them on the doorframes of your houses and on your gates.

Deuteronomy 6:4–9

Beliefs and teachings

So if you faithfully obey the commands I am giving you today – to love the Lord your God and to serve him with all your heart and with all your soul – then I will send rain on your land in its season, both autumn and spring rains, so that you may gather in your grain, new wine and oil. I will provide grass in the fields for your cattle, and you will eat and be satisfied.

Be careful, or you will be enticed to turn away and worship other gods and bow down to them. Then the Lord's anger will burn against you, and he will shut the heavens so that it will not rain and the ground will yield no produce, and you will soon perish from the good land the Lord is giving you. Fix these words of mine in your hearts and minds; tie them as symbols on your hands and bind them on your foreheads. Teach them to your children, talking about them when you sit at home and when you walk along the road, when you lie down and when you get up. Write them on the doorframes of your houses and on your gates, so that your days and the days of your children may be many in the land that the Lord swore to give your forefathers, as many as the days that the heavens are above the earth.

Deuteronomy 11:13-21

AQA Examiner's tip

You should learn the main beliefs that are contained in the Shema – it may help to learn by heart some short phrases of the Shema.

All your heart – Jews believe that God requires absolute loyalty, just like a marriage.

All your soul – Jews believe that God requires total spiritual dedication.

All your strength – this way of serving God demands the dedication of money and physical strength. Jews believe that in order to love God, they should constantly appreciate that any material possessions such as money or property of any sort are a direct gift from God. By giving to charity, Jews believe that they are serving God.

Teach them diligently – Jews believe that by learning the words of God, the Torah – they are able to pass on the teachings to their children, and in doing so continue the tradition of Jewish education.

It is important to understand that Jews believe the Torah is so important that a person should be occupied with it wherever and whenever they can.

B *Jews believe that every aspect of the world and its contents is controlled by God*

Activities

1 What do Jews believe about the importance of Jewish education?

2 Read through a translation of the Shema and then make a list of the commandments that are contained in it.

3 Find out as much information as you can about mezuzah and tefillin. What is the importance of these objects for Jews and how are they connected with the Shema?

4 Look at the second paragraph of the Shema (opposite). Write down both sides of the Covenant described in it.

Summary

You should now know about the Shema, and what it tells Jews about the unity of God.

שלה ח מיי' פ"ה מל'
ממריס כלכס '
מוש"ע י"ד סי'רמ סעי'נ:

דלא מפקידינא ועבדינא · מכאן
מדקדק ר"ה דנשיס מברכות
על מלות עשה שהזמן גרמא אע"ג
דפטורות לגמרי דאפילו מדרבנן לא

שיהלך ארבע אמות בקומה זקופה שנא'
יי°מלא כל הארץ כבודו רב הונא בריה דרב
יהושע 'לא מסגי ארבע אמות בגילוי הראש
אמר שבינה למעלה מראשי שאל בן אלמנה

לעשות אמר לי אבא ואימא הטיט
בלשון שחוק : חורו וסודו למאמרוס
סרלסונוס · כ"ש שחייב אדם בכבודו
שאף הוא שותף בבריאתו כאביו ואמו

1.5 God the creator and sustainer

God the creator

The opening verses of the Torah state the belief that God created the universe out of nothing. This belief is known as 'something out of nothing'. In this way, Jews regard the world as having been created by God according to a precise plan. By understanding the whole act of creation as coming from nothing, Jews accept that God created the world exactly as he wanted it to be.

It is very difficult to understand the concept of 'something out of nothing' fully. Think about someone trying to make their thoughts a reality – perhaps someone deciding to think about creating a bunch of flowers. We could see, smell and touch them, and they would be very real. However, as soon as we stop thinking about the flowers, they would cease to exist. In other words, the flowers are only there because we think about them.

A 'In the beginning God created the heavens and the earth'

The appreciation of the role of God as **creator** of the universe is often challenged by the fact that one of the fundamental principles is that God is without a body or bodily form. Although it is impossible to imagine what God looks like, Jews believe that God has three very important basic characteristics.

- Omnipotent – God is all powerful.
- Omniscience – God is all knowing.
- Omnipresent – God is everywhere.

This idea that God is capable of doing everything and anything goes hand in hand with the concept that God holds back his power and allows humans the freedom to choose the way that they wish to live on Earth. This is known as 'free choice' or 'free will'. It is believed that God, through miracles, does occasionally intervene in earthly affairs, but generally Jews believe that by allowing humans free choice, God allows humans to develop spiritually and to grow according to his divine plan.

Objectives

Understand God as creator and sustainer.

Key terms

Creator: (the belief that) God created everything.

Sustainer: (the belief that) God provides food and natural resources for the world.

Activities

1 Explain the concept of free will within God's plan for the world.

2 'We don't really have free choice; God controls all our lives.' Do you agree? Give reasons to support your answer and show you understand both sides of the argument.

God the sustainer

God is viewed as not only creating the entire world, but also providing food and natural resources to feed and sustain humankind. This aspect of God as the sustainer of the world is acknowledged by Jews when they recite Grace after every meal.

> 66 *For He is God who feeds and sustains all, does good to all, and prepares food for all creatures He has created. Blessed are You, Lord who feeds all.* 99
>
> Grace after Meals
> Authorised Daily Prayer Book

The idea of God as a **sustainer** is sometimes difficult to understand, especially when people think of famine and world poverty. However, it is necessary to remember the concept of free choice or free will. Jews believe that God does provide enough food to sustain the entire world, but it remains the basic responsibility of the human race to ensure that this food is distributed fairly across the world.

By exercising free choice and reaching out and helping those in need, Jews believe that they are fulfilling God's plan for the world.

B *We have a responsibility to fulfil God's role as sustainer by looking after others*

Case study

A place to pray

Travellers visiting the famous Niagara Falls in the USA noticed with interest the presence of an old man, who by his appearance was obviously a Hasidic Jew. He was standing on a viewing platform, praying devoutly. When approached and asked why he chose this place to pray, he sincerely replied that he was merely offering praise to God for the beauty of creation.

Activity

3 Read the case study. How does this story illustrate the Jewish belief in God as creator?

Discussion activity 👤👤👤

With a partner or in a small group, discuss how Jews can believe that God is the sustainer of the world, when there is famine and hardship in the world.

C *The Niagra falls was an inspiration for prayer and thanks to God*

Summary

You should now understand the Jewish idea of God as creator and sustainer of all things.

AQA *Examiner's tip*

Make sure you understand what is meant by describing God as creator and sustainer.

ממריס הלכה · י
מדקדק כ"ח דנשים מברכות
על מלות עשה שהזמן גרמא אע"ג
דפטורות לגמרי דאפילו מדרבנן לא

דלא מפקידנא ועבדינא · מכאן
מוט"ע י"ד סילם סעי"ג:
שלו פ' ועוט"ע שם
סעי' ה:

שׁיהֵךְ אַרְבַּע אַמּוֹת בְּקוֹמָה זְקוּפָה שֶׁנֶּא
יּמְלֵא כָל הָאָרֶץ כְּבוֹדוֹ רַב הוּנָא בְּרֵיהּ דְּרַב
יְהוֹשֻׁעַ יּלֹא מְסַנֵּי אַרְבַּע אַמּוֹת בְּגִילוּי הָרֹאשׁ
אָמַר שְׁכִינָה לְמַעְלָה מֵרֹאשִׁי שְׁאַל בֶּן אַלְמָנָה

לְעְשׂוֹת אָמַר לִי אבא וְאִמָּא הֵיטִיבוּ
בְּלְשׁוֹן שָׂחוּק : זוֹרְזוֹ וְסוֹדוֹ לַמְּאַמְּרוֹת
מִדְּאֹסְלֵמוֹנוֹס · כ"ש שָׂחִיב אָדָם בִּכְבוֹדוֹ
שֶׁאֵן הוּא שׁוּתָּף בְּבְרִיאָתוֹ כְּאָבִיו וְאִמּוֹ

1.6 God the law giver and judge, redeemer and sanctifier

God the giver of the law

One of the most basic of all Jewish beliefs is that God gave the Torah to Moses on Mount Sinai. The Torah is the most holy of all Jewish writings and is the source of 613 mitzvoth or commandments that form the basis of Halakhah. Jewish people believe that by obeying the laws and commandments they are fulfilling God's will on earth and, in doing so, forming a close relationship with him.

One aspect of this belief is that just as God has given Jews his law, he also will judge Jews on the way that they have kept the mitzvoth.

There is a very descriptive account of the process that surrounded the giving of the law to the Jewish people. This is found in the collection of Rabbinic writings known as midrash. This states that God wished to give Torah to the world. He approached different nations and offered the Torah to each in turn. Each nation enquired as to the contents of the Torah, and when informed of the restrictions, decided to refuse. When God approached the Jews, they replied 'we will do and we will listen'.

This shows the way in which Jews accept the Torah as a gift from God without any conditions.

The Ten Commandments

Jews believe that the Ten Commandments were given by God at Mount Sinai to the entire Jewish nation. No other nation claims to have had a revelation to a nation in this way, and Jews believe that the commandments form a basic covenant or agreement between God and the Jews. If Jews keep the details of the commandments, they will live in a society that is close to God.

The Commandments were inscribed on two tablets of stone, and comprise two groups of statements. The first five statements are between man and God, and the second are between man and man. By placing both groups side by side, Jews believe that both sets of Commandments are of equal importance.

The Ten Commandments: Exodus 20:2–17

1 You shall have no other god before me
2 You shall not make for yourself an idol
3 You shall not misuse the name of the Lord your God
4 Remember the Sabbath day by keeping it holy
5 Honour your father and mother
6 You shall not murder
7 You shall not commit adultery
8 You shall not steal
9 You shall not give false testimony against your neighbour
10 You shall not covet (be jealous of) your neighbour's house … or anything that belongs to your neighbour

A The Ten Commandments are a focal point in every synagogue and are usually found placed above the Ark

Discussion activity ■■■

Can a person be a good Jew if they do not keep all of the commandments? Discuss.

AQA Examiner's tip

Make sure that you know the Ten Commandments. You do not have to learn the longer ones off by heart but you need to know the main meaning of them.

The Ten Commandments form an important part of Jewish worship. They are read formally in synagogue as part of the regular cycle of Torah readings, as well as on the festival of Shavuot (Pentecost), which among other things celebrates the giving of the law on Mount Sinai.

God the judge

Jews believe that God not only gave the world his law, but that he also constantly judges the behaviour of every person. This is illustrated by the fact that one of the major Jewish festivals, Rosh Hashanah, provides Jews with an opportunity to repent and reflect on their behaviour, and to pray for goodness and happiness for themselves and their families.

God the redeemer

The concept of God as the redeemer of Israel is a very important one for Jews. It is a fundamental belief in Judaism that God will always save or redeem his people, especially at times of crisis.

This is reflected in the Siddur (the Jewish book of prayer), where the central Amidah prayer is always preceded by a blessing, which praises God as the redeemer of Israel.

> 66 *Rock of Israel! Arise to the help of Israel. Deliver, as you promised Judah and Israel. Our Redeemer is the Lord of hosts … blessed are You Lord, who redeemed Israel.* 99

The belief in God as the redeemer is also included in the final sentence of the Shema prayer, where God identifies himself as having saved the people of Israel from slavery in Egypt:

> 66 *I am the Lord your God who brought you out of the land of Egypt to be your God …* 99

Jews believe that the gratitude due to God who redeemed them is a vital part of their worship, and one that will strengthen their loyalty to him.

God the sanctifier

Jews believe that the act of sanctification – becoming holy – is achieved by fulfilling the mitzvoth, the commandments that God gave to them. This belief is underlined by a famous quotation in the Torah:

Beliefs and teachings

You shall be holy for I the Lord your God am holy.

Leviticus 19

The meaning of this sentence is plain. By performing mitzvoth, Jews believe that they are fulfilling the divine plan that God has for them – to become a holy nation. They believe that by fulfilling these commandments they are undergoing a process of sanctification – becoming holy.

One of the most important ways a Jew can become holy is by helping another person who is in need. This could be by giving charity, or helping in any way that is of benefit to a person. The word for this is tzedakah – an act of righteousness.

B   *Giving charity*

Activities

1. Write your own version of the Ten Commandments, putting each one into a modern context.

2. Why do you think that the commandment honouring parents is placed within the group of commandments honouring God?

3. 'It is too difficult to keep every commandment today – we need to alter them to suit modern times.' Do you agree? Try to show different opinions in your answer.

Extension activity

Research Exodus 21 and write down three mitzvoth (commandments) that deal with the correct way to treat one another.

Summary

You should now understand the Jewish belief in God as law giver and judge.

You should also understand the way that God is viewed as the saviour or redeemer of Israel, and how performing mitzvoth helps Jews to become more holy.

1.7 The Covenant

◼ What is a covenant?

The word covenant is best seen as a way of understanding God's relationship with man. It can be understood as an agreement between two parties, which benefits each. Both parties to the agreement have to fulfil obligations or duties if the covenant is to be considered binding. A good example of this kind of agreement is that of a mortgage arrangement, which can be agreed with a bank or building society.

The bank or building society will lend money to a person so that they can purchase a house and, in return, the borrower will agree to repay the loan with interest, so that the lender will make a profit.

If either party fails to honour their side of the contract, then the arrangement will be cancelled.

Discussion activity 👥👥

Can you think of any other types of binding agreements that exist in the world today? Discuss this with a partner.

However, the arrangement for a mortgage is in the form of a contract, which, unlike a covenant, only lasts as long as both parties are enjoying the benefits of the relationship. A covenant, on the other hand, is a commitment of love and creates a relationship that is fundamentally different from that of a contract. Covenants in Judaism can only be established and sealed by an oath. The oath is so important in a covenant that the word oath is sometimes used as a synonym for covenant.

The Covenant with God is described as 'an everlasting covenant' (brit olam). This describes the view that God will never break his covenant agreement with the Jewish people, even if, from time to time, they fail to fulfil their covenant obligations and break his laws. In the Torah, God is described as 'remembering the covenant that he made with Abraham, Isaac and Jacob'. This is evidence of the unbreakable bond of covenant love that God has with the Jewish people.

Objectives

Examine the Jewish belief in Israel as God's chosen people.

A *A covenant can be viewed as a mutually beneficial agreement*

Key terms

The Covenant: God's agreement to look after the Jews as his chosen people, subject to Israel's obedience.

Israel: the ancient name for the Jewish people.

Beliefs and teachings

For you are a holy people to the Lord your God, and the Lord has chosen you out of all peoples that are on the face of the earth.

Deuteronomy 14:2

Jews, the people of **Israel**, are sometimes referred to as the 'Chosen People'. This description has caused problems in some ways, because it gives the impression that Jews are in some way superior as a nation. A more accurate way of understanding this title is to realise that Jews think of themselves as being chosen for responsibility, and not for superiority.

Jews understand and believe that all nations of the earth have a basic obligation to serve God by obeying the Noachide Covenant.

The Noachide Covenant that was established after the flood was a set of seven obligations for all mankind to keep. In this way society would become more structured and eventually a much more civilised place. Jewish people believe that all Gentile – non-Jewish – societies have a basic obligation to fulfil the seven Noachide laws in order to be accepted into heaven. The Noachide Covenant was important because it was the first time that the responsibility for justice was given to mankind. Up to that point in history, any justice that was necessary was administered by God.

<aside>
Extension activity

Look up the Noachide Laws in Genesis 9:4.
</aside>

<aside>
AQA   Examiner's tip

It is a good idea to look at the basic details of the covenant that God concluded with Noah, but you will not be tested on this in the examination.
</aside>

B   *The rainbow is a symbol for God's covenant with Noah*

Research activity

Use the internet to find out more about the Noachide laws, and write down all seven laws.

Activities

1   Explain what you understand by the term covenant.
2   How do Jews view their relationship with God through the Covenants?
3   Why do you think the Noachide Covenant was important for society in general?

<aside>
Summary

You should now understand the Jewish belief in Israel as God's chosen people, and know about the Covenant between God and Jews.
</aside>

שלה ח מיי' פ* מני'
מדקדק ר\"ה נבטים מברכות
על מלות עשה שהומן גרמא אנ\"ג
דפטורות נגמרי דאפי«לו מדרבנן לא

דלא מפקידנא ועבדינא · מכאן
מוש\"ע י\"ד סילמ סע\"ב:
שלו ם מוש\"ע שם
סעי\"ד ה:

שיהלך ארבע אמות בקומה זקופה שנא'
ם י\"מלא כל הארץ כבודו רב הונא בריה דרב
יהושע לא מסני ארבע אמות בגילוי הראש
אמר שבינה למעלה מראשי שאל בן אלמנה

לנשות אמר לי אבא ואימא הטיט
בלשון שחוק : חורו וסורו למאמרות
סראשונות · כ\"ש שחייב אדם בכבודו
אף הוא שותקן בכביאתו כאביו ואמו

1.8 The Covenant with Abraham

▇ Abraham – the first Jew

Jewish tradition believes that Abraham was born in the city of Ur in Mesopotamia in approximately 1800 BCE. His father, Terach, was a man who made his living by selling idols, but from his early childhood, Abraham became convinced of the presence in the world of a higher power. He came to believe that the universe was the creative work of a single divine Creator. He began to spread this belief to other people and in doing so became the first believer in the idea of monotheism (belief in one god).

An ancient Midrashic commentary describes how Abraham tried to convince his father Terach of the futility of idol worship.

Objectives

Understand what is meant by the Covenant with Abraham and why Jews believe it to be important.

Case study

Abraham

One day, when Abraham was left alone to look after his father's shop, he took a hammer and smashed all of the idols except the largest one. He placed the hammer in the hand of the largest idol. When his father returned and asked what happened, Abraham said, 'The idols got into a fight, and the big one smashed all the other ones.' His father said, 'Don't be ridiculous. These idols have no life or power. They can't do anything.' Abraham replied, 'Then why do you worship them?'

Activity

1 Write out your own account of the famous story of Abraham and his father's idols. Write from the point of view of Abraham.

Activity

2 You can find the account of Abraham's journey to Canaan in Genesis 12. Imagine you are Abraham – write a diary recording the momentous events of your journey to Canaan. You can use Map B to help you.

A *The long journey to Canaan*

The Torah in Genesis 12 describes how God spoke to Abraham and commanded him to abandon his old life in Mesopotamia and to travel to the land of Canaan – later to be known as Israel. There, God promised him, Abraham would be the founder of a great nation. God would bless him and would protect him from any harmful nations. Abraham accepted this offer and sealed the covenant by circumcising himself and all the males in his family. This aspect of the covenant has become known as 'The Covenant of Abraham our father'.

We have seen that the idea of a covenant is regarded as an important part of traditional Judaism. Jews believe that they have a Covenant with God, which involves rights and obligations on both sides. Abraham was subjected to ten tests of faith to convince God that he was worthy to accept the covenant. Obeying the command to leave home was the first of these tests.

The Torah records how, at the age of 75, Abraham, together with his wife Sarah, his nephew Lot and all his household, left his birthplace in Mesopotamia to travel to Canaan, which God had promised to Abraham's descendants.

Beliefs and teachings

'And God spoke to Abraham … go from your land, your birthplace, from your father's house, to a land that I will show you.'

Genesis 12: 2–3

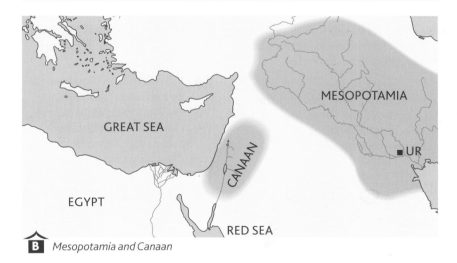

B *Mesopotamia and Canaan*

Activities

3 Why do Jews regard the Covenant with God as an important part of their tradition?

4 Which part of the covenant with Abraham do you think Jews regard as the most important?

Summary

You should now understand the Covenant with Abraham and its significance.

∞ links

Find out more about Jewish beliefs about circumcision on pages 102–103.

Research activity 🔍

Research and list the ten tests that God sent Abraham.

AQA Examiner's tip

Learn the details of the covenant with Abraham and summarise the significance of this for Jews.

1.9 The centrality of the Torah to the Covenant

Objectives

Understand the central role of the Torah to the Covenant.

A Simchat Torah is marked by singing and dancing as the Torah scrolls are carried around

Celebrating the Torah

One of the happiest of all Jewish festivals is known as Simchat Torah. This marks the completion of the yearly cycle of reading the Torah with the last verses of Deuteronomy and the beginning of the first verses of Genesis. In all synagogues, Simchat Torah is a festive occasion, marked by singing and dancing as the Torah scrolls are carried in festive procession around the synagogue.

Jews feel that the importance given to the festival shows how central the Torah is to Judaism. They believe that without the Torah the Covenant with God would lack any real meaning. The Torah is so important to Jews that, throughout their history, thousands of Jews have lived and died by its teachings.

The Torah is vitally important as a way that Jews can continue their long history and tradition. This is shown by the following:

- Jews still read from the same Hebrew Torah text that they have used for over 2,000 years.
- Jews have studied and commented on every phrase and word of the Torah.
- The last letter of the Torah is a 'lamed' and the first letter is a 'bet' (pronounced 'v'), which spell out the word 'lev' meaning heart. This reminds Jews that the Torah is the heart of Judaism.
- The Torah contains the details of the covenant between God and the Jewish people.
- The revelation of God to the Jews on Mount Sinai, and the giving of the Torah to the Jewish people, was witnessed by the entire Jewish nation.

Activities

1. Summarise the reasons that Jews give for regarding the Torah as an important part of their lives.

2. 'Life without the Torah would be meaningless for Jews.' Do you agree? Write out the main points of a discussion that people with different opinions would have.

- According to Jewish tradition (see quotation below), the Torah is one of the three things that sustain the world.
- According to the Talmud, the Torah begins and ends with an act of loving kindness.
- The Torah is regarded as the source of all mitzvoth – commandments that form the Halakhah. It is this that Jews follow as part of their daily lives.

B *The revelation of God on Mount Sinai was witnessed by the entire Jewish nation*

> 66 *The Torah begins with an act of loving kindness, God clothing Adam and Eve, and ends with an act of loving kindness: God burying Moses.* 99
>
> *Talmud Sotah 14a*

In this way Jews view the Torah as the basis for every aspect of their lives. The covenant that is so important to Jewish life is centred on the values of the Torah, and keeping to the Torah is regarded as the basic demand of the covenant.

The fact that the entire nation of Israel was witness to the revelation on Mount Sinai is a fundamental aspect of Jewish belief. The obligation to accept the teachings of the Torah was made unconditionally by the entire nation of Israel as they stood at the foot of Mount Sinai just before the revelation.

Beliefs and teachings

We will do everything the Lord has said.

Exodus 1 9:8

By accepting the words of God as one nation, Jews believe that the everlasting covenant that God made with them was fixed and strengthened. Even if Jews as individuals choose not to follow all the words of the covenant, they accept that as a nation, they are still bound by the promises made in it.

Summary

You should now understand how the Torah is a central aspect of every Jew's life. Without the values of the Torah, Jews believe that the Covenant would lack any real meaning.

Jews feel that following the teachings of the Torah is part of the chain of tradition that goes back thousands of years.

Beliefs and teachings

Simon the Just used to say … on three things the world rests … On Torah, on the service of God and on acts of loving kindness.

Ethics of the Fathers Chapter 1:2

Research activity

Research the account of the giving of the Torah in Exodus 19 and 20, and then write out the account in your own words.

Extension activity

Use the internet to find out about the weekly cycle of Torah reading. Try to write out the details of the portion that is being read this week.

Discussion activity

'The laws of the Torah are out of date and have little relevance today.' Discuss this viewpoint in a group.

דלא מפקידנא ועבדינא · מכאן
מדקדק ר"ת דנשים מברכות
על מצות עשה שהזמן גרמא אע"ג
דפטורות נגמרי דאפילו מדרבנן לא

שיהלך ארבע אמות בקומה זקופה שנא'
שם י°מלא כל הארץ כבודו רב הונא בריה דרב
יהושע ילא מסני ארבע אמות בגילוי הראש
אמר שבינה למעלה מראשי שאל בן אלמנה

1.10 The Messianic Age

Messiah – the anointed one

A *Jews pray every day for the coming of the messiah*

Messiah (Moshiach) means 'anointed one' and is the expression found in the Tenakh to describe the kings of Israel who, in a ceremony of being recognised as the king, were anointed with holy olive oil.

Today, the term messiah has come to be understood by Jews to be a reference to a future King of Israel who will be a descendant of King David and who will rule the Jewish people during the Messianic Age. Orthodox Jews include a prayer, which they say at the end of the morning weekday service, in which they pray for the speedy arrival of the Messiah.

The Messianic Age

The Messianic Age itself is described by the prophet Micah as a time when war will end and all people will enjoy universal peace and harmony. The words of the prophet are a stirring reminder of the vision of peace that all men and women seek.

> ❝ *They shall beat their swords into ploughshares and spears into pruning hooks, nation will not take up sword against nation, nor will they train for war anymore.* ❞
>
> *Micah 4:3*

Indeed these words form an important engraving on the side of the United Nations building in New York.

B *The statue outside the UN building in New York, inspired by Micah 4:3*

Traditional Jewish thought includes a belief that the Messiah will be a direct descendant of King David who will be responsible for gathering the Jews back to the Land of Israel, and will also bring about world peace and understanding between nations.

Orthodox Jews believe that they are obliged to accept and uphold the 13 Principles of Faith. This creed was written by the medieval Jewish rabbi and philosopher Moses Maimonedes. One of these principles refers to the belief in the coming of the Messiah:

> 66 *I believe with perfect faith in the coming of the Moshiach, and even though he tarries, with all of that I await his arrival with every day.* 99
>
> *13 Principles of Jewish Faith*

The belief in the coming of the Messiah has helped to sustain Jews through some of the darkest periods in their history. Many Jews went to their deaths in the Nazi death camps with those words on their lips. The belief in a messiah who would make the world a place of peace and harmony has been a sustaining one throughout Jewish history.

Research activity

Using the library or the internet, research the prophecies about the coming of a Messiah.

Auschwitz, July 1944

A group of Hungarian Hasidic Jews were waiting in line to enter the gas chambers. As they filed slowly towards their final destiny, the guards who were supervising them were surprised to hear the sound of singing, quiet at first and then gradually rising in volume to a powerful crescendo. Bystanders and witnesses later reported that the words of the song were those sung every day by Jews, 'I believe with perfect faith in the coming of the Messiah, and even though he tarries, I await his arrival.'

Try to understand the meaning behind this incident and how it represented a basic Jewish belief.

C

Case study

Activities

1 Describe how the belief in the messiah has sustained Jews throughout their history, especially at difficult and dangerous times.

2 Summarise the different opinions regarding the Messiah that are held by different Jewish denominations.

3 'It is no use waiting for the Messiah; we should work together to bring peace ourselves.' Discuss this statement in a group.

Summary

You should now know about the Jewish belief in the Messiah and understand the importance of this belief to Jews.

AQA *Examiner's tip*

It is important to learn the Jewish view of the Messiah and to understand the central importance that Jews place on this belief.

You should also understand the various different views about the Messiah that different Jewish groups hold.

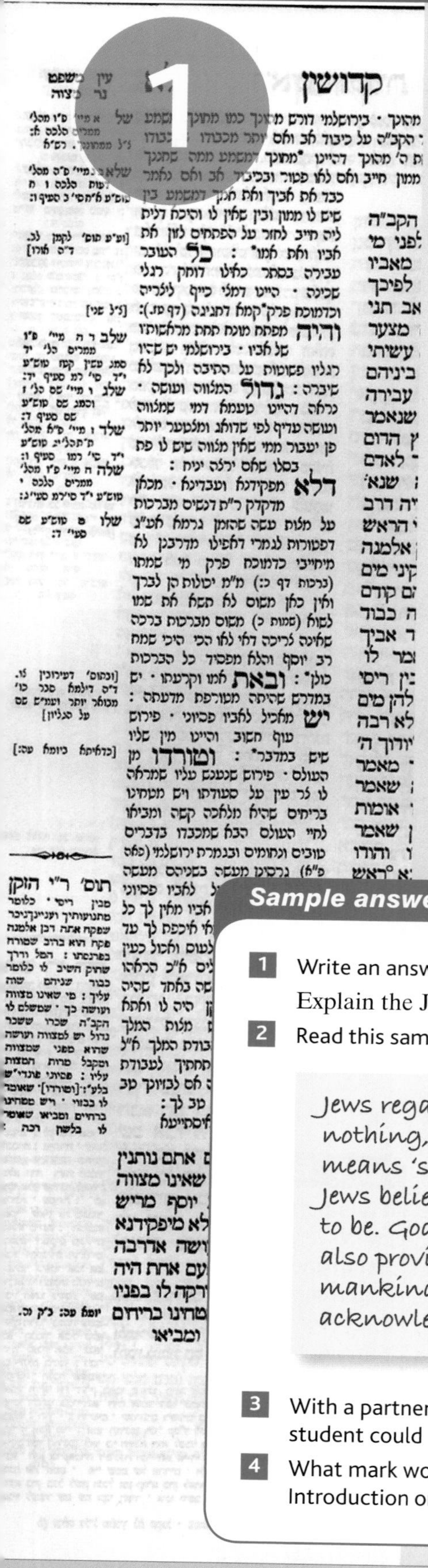

קדושין

Beliefs and sources of authority – summary

For the examination you should be able to:

✔ know and understand the key beliefs and sources of authority that underpin the Jewish way of life, and influence behaviour and attitudes

✔ know and understand Jewish views on

  – the *Torah*, *Neviim* and *Ketuvim*

  – the Talmud: the Mishnah and Gemara

  – Halakhah, Bet Din, Responsa and yeshivah

✔ understand and be able to discuss Jewish concepts of God including

  – the unity of God; the Shema

  – God as creator and sustainer

  – God as law giver and judge

  – God as redeemer and sanctifier

✔ know and understand the Jewish view of the Covenant including

  – Israel as God's chosen people.

  – the Covenant with Abraham

  – the centrality of the Torah (written and oral) to the Covenant

  – the Messianic Age

Sample answer

1 Write an answer to the following exam question.

Explain the Jewish view of God as creator and sustainer. *(6 marks)*

2 Read this sample answer.

> Jews regard the world as having been created by God from nothing, according to a precise plan. The Hebrew word for this idea means 'something from nothing'. By accepting this principle, Jews believe that God created the world exactly as he wanted it to be. God is viewed as not only creating the entire world, but also providing food and natural resources to feed and sustain mankind. This aspect of God as the sustainer of the world is acknowledged by Jews when they recite Grace after every meal.

3 With a partner, discuss this sample answer. Do you think that there are other things the student could have included in their answer?

4 What mark would you give this answer out of six? Look at the mark scheme in the Introduction on page 7 (AO1). What are the reasons for the mark that you have given?

AQA Examination-style questions

1 Look at the photograph below and answer the following questions.

(a) Explain briefly what is meant by the term 'Halakhah'? *(2 marks)*

Only two marks are available so you do not have to give a long, detailed explanation.

(b) Explain Jewish beliefs about the way Halakhah can help with problems of life in society today. *(4 marks)*

To gain full marks here you need to show a clear knowledge and understanding of Jewish teachings about Halakhah. It may be helpful to include examples in your answer to clarify the points you make.

(c) 'The Bet Din interferes too much in personal matters.' Do you agree? Give reasons for your answer, showing that you have thought about more than one point of view. Refer to Jewish teaching in your answer. *(6 marks)*

You can agree, disagree or be undecided about these statements. Remember that you must give reasons to support more than one point of view.

(d) Explain the importance of the Jewish belief in the Messiah. *(6 marks)*

Here you will need to show that you understand the importance of the Jewish belief in the Messiah.

(e) 'Halakhah is old fashioned and no longer relevant for the 21st century.' Do you agree? Give reasons for your answer showing that you have thought about more than one point of view. Refer to Jewish teachings in your answer. *(6 marks)*

In these longer evaluation questions it is worth spending a few moments planning out how you are going to structure your response. Remember to include more than one point of view.

2 The synagogue and worship

2.1 Worship in Judaism

Beliefs and teachings

Praise the Lord.

Praise God in his sanctuary;

praise him in his mighty heavens.

Praise him for his acts of power;

praise him for his surpassing greatness.

Praise him with the sounding of the trumpet,

praise him with the harp and lyre,

praise him with tambourine and dancing,

praise him with the strings and flute,

praise him with the clash of cymbals,

praise him with resounding cymbals.

Let everything that has breath praise the Lord.

Praise the Lord.

Psalm 150

Activities

1 Read Psalm 150 that may be used as part of Jewish morning worship.

2 Write an explanation of what the Psalm tells Jews about God and how God should be worshipped.

Worship in Judaism

Jews **worship** one God, with whom they believe that they have a special relationship. All aspects of Jewish life are seen as ways to show love and obedience to God: an opportunity to worship God. These Jewish beliefs have an influence on private worship at home and in the synagogue. Often, objects are used to help Jews focus their attention in worship, such as special items of clothing.

Although Jews share a belief about the importance of worship, there are a number of branches that have developed within Judaism that have different understandings as to the form that worship should take. Two main divisions that have resulted in differences in synagogue design and the form of worship are the Orthodox tradition and Reform Judaism. These are the two divisions that will be used as examples of different practices within Judaism in this chapter.

Jews are required to pray three times a day and this will often take place in the home. Home worship also involves obeying the laws found in the Torah, and this includes the dietary laws. The most important

Objectives

Know and understand what is meant by worship in Judaism.

A *A synagogue in Israel*

Key terms

Worship: a specific act of religious devotion.

∞links

If you are not sure what is meant by a synagogue, read the definition of a synagogue on page 36 of this chapter.

If you are not sure of the role of a rabbi, read the definition of a rabbi on page 48 of this chapter.

∞links

For more information about beliefs and authority in Judaism see Chapter 1, pages 8–27.

The Western Wall in Jerusalem is a place of great significance and a pilgrimage site for Jews. Read 3.9, pages 68–69 to find out why.

worship that takes place in the Jewish home and synagogue occurs each Sabbath and on festival and holy days.

The Orthodox tradition

Orthodox Jews believe that the Torah is to be taken literally as it is God's direct word. Therefore the laws contained within in it must still be kept according to the interpretation of it as found in the Talmud. Orthodox Jews believe that they are to preserve the traditional worship as received from the rabbis of the past, as this is the worship based on God's instructions in the Torah. Hebrew is the sacred language of Judaism and the language in which the scriptures are written, and therefore this is the language that must be used in worship to ensure that there is the correct understanding of the scriptures as sent by God. Men and women sit separately in Orthodox synagogues to avoid distractions during worship as the focus of worship must be God. There is a concern that men may not give their full concentration to their prayers if women are present. There are only male rabbis in the Orthodox tradition. This is because Orthodox Jews believe that God has given a clear instruction that this role may only be undertaken by a man. Orthodox Jews are expected to walk to the synagogue on the Sabbath because of the rules of Sabbath observance that they believe must be kept. Singing in an Orthodox synagogue is unaccompanied and Jews stand for some of the prayers for part of the service to show that they are above the animals and as devotion to God.

Reform Judaism

Reform Jews want to retain as much as possible of the traditions of Judaism but at the same time make the faith more relevant to modern life. Reform Jews do not believe that the Torah has to be taken literally as it was inspired by God but is not God's direct word. For Reform Jews, it is the spiritual and moral code within the Torah and Talmud that must be obeyed, not each individual law. It is therefore acceptable to change the way in which God is worshipped as they regard Judaism as an evolving religion that adapts to modern life. This means that most Reform Jews will travel by car to the synagogue for Sabbath worship. Women and men sit together for worship in a Reform synagogue and take an active part in the service, as the Reform tradition believes that God has given them equal status in worship. The service may be led by a woman rabbi. In a Reform synagogue most parts of the service are in the worshipper's own language. Singing is often accompanied by an organ in Reform synagogues.

Activity

3   Read Chapter 4, pages 82–83, in which it is explained how the rules of Sabbath observance are applied to modern activities.

Based on that reasoning, explain why Orthodox Jews are expected to walk to the synagogue on the Sabbath.

Activities

4   What is a synagogue?
5   Explain the major differences in worship between Orthodox and Reform Jews.

B   *Jews praying near the Western Wall in Jerusalem*

AQA   *Examiner's tip*

Make sure that you are able to explain the differences in worship between Orthodox and Reform Jews.

The Western (Wailing) Wall in Jerusalem

The Western Wall is all that remains to mark the site of King Herod's Temple that was destroyed by the Romans in 70 CE. It is sometimes called the Wailing Wall on account of the sorrowful prayers said there, mourning the loss of the Temple. Herod's Temple was the second temple, and was built on the site of the Solomon's Temple which had housed the Ark of the Covenant, the sacred chest that contained the tablets inscribed with the Ten Commandments that were given to Moses by God. Solomon's Temple was destroyed in 587 BCE by the Babylonians and the Ark was lost.

Case study

Summary

You should now be able to explain what is meant by worship in Judaism, and explain some of the major differences between the worship of Orthodox and Reform Jews.

Symbols of prayer

When Jewish men pray they wear two visible symbols of prayer, the **tallit** and **tefillin**, to help remind them of their relationship with God and the importance of prayer. Jews believe that they have been commanded in the Torah to wear such items and therefore, by wearing them, they are obeying God's command. By continuing the tradition of wearing the tallit and tefillin, established at the time of Moses, Jews are made aware of their long history, their special relationship with God and the covenant, part of which is a promise to keep God's laws.

When they put on the tallit and tefillin, Jews feel that they are dressing for what is important: that is the worship of God and this helps them to focus on their prayers. In the Orthodox Jewish tradition, the tallit and tefillin are only worn by men but in the Reform tradition women may wear them as well.

Beliefs and teachings

Speak to the Israelites and say to them:
'Throughout the generations to come you are
to make tassels on the corners of your garments,
with a blue cord on each tassel. You will have these
tassels to look at and so you will remember all the
commands of the Lord, that you may obey them
and not prostitute yourselves by going after the lusts
of your own hearts and eyes. Then you will remember
to obey all my commands and will be consecrated to
your God.

Numbers 15:38–40

Tallit

The tallit is a prayer shawl with a total of 613 long fringes called tzitzit attached to the corners. The tzitzit are the most important part of the tallit, as they are a reminder of the laws from God that Jews are expected to obey. The tallit is white and usually made of wool, cotton or silk, but it cannot be made from a combination of wool and linen as this combination is forbidden for clothing in Judaism. The tallit must be large enough to go over the wearer's shoulders. It may have blue or black stripes woven across each end just above the fringes. The tallit is worn for morning prayers, Sabbath worship and holy days. Some Jews wear a small tallit called the tallit katan all day under their clothes, but not next to the skin, as a reminder of God's laws that they need to keep. Jews believe that by wearing this shawl they are obeying the instruction in Numbers 15:38–40.

Objectives

Know and understand the symbolism and function of the tallit and tefillin in Judaism.

Evaluate the importance of wearing special clothes for worship.

Key terms

Tallit: a prayer shawl.

Tefillin: small leather boxes containing extracts from the Torah, strapped to the believer's arms and forehead for morning prayers.

A A tallit

Tallits are often given as gifts at significant times in a Jew's life. For example, boys are given a tallit at their Bar Mitzvah, and a bridegroom will wear his tallit at his wedding.

Tefillin

The tefillin are black leather boxes with straps attached that are sometimes called phylacteries. Before saying the morning prayers, Jews will strap one of the tefillin on their arm and the other on their forehead. As Jews pray, the arm with the box is placed across the chest so that the word of God enters both the head and the heart of the believer. The tefillin are not worn on Shabbat or during festival days. Inside the tefillin are handwritten passages from the Torah.

Research activity

Using a copy of the Torah or the Old Testament write out these four passages: Exodus 13:1–10, 11–16; Deuteronomy 6:4–9, 11:13–21, which are the handwritten passages found in the tefillin.

Why do you think that it is these passages that are found in the tefillin? Explain your opinion.

B *Jews wear tefillin for prayer*

Activities

1 Describe the tallit and tefillin used in Jewish worship.

2 Explain how the tallit and tefillin are used in Jewish worship.

3 Explain the meaning of the symbolism of the tallit and tefillin.

4 'Wearing special clothes for worship helps worshippers to concentrate.' What do you think? Explain your opinion.

Discussion activity

With a partner, in a group or as a whole class discuss the benefits and disadvantages of wearing special clothing when prayers are said.

Summary

You should now be able to explain the symbolism and function of the tallit and tefillin in Judaism and have evaluated the idea of having special clothes for worship.

 Examiner's tip

Make sure that you are able to explain exactly how the tallit and tefillin are used by Jews in prayer.

The minyan

The word **minyan** means 'count' or 'number'. In Judaism, the minyan is the minimum number of ten Jews that are needed to be together for certain acts of worship to take place, for example public worship in the synagogue and for the study of the Law. In Orthodox Judaism the requirement is ten men over 13 years of age, whereas in Reform Judaism, adult women can be included in the minyan. The minyan will usually hold a service in the synagogue but can meet elsewhere.

Objectives

Investigate what is meant by the minyan in Judaism.

Key terms

Minyan: a quorum of ten men (or adults in Reform Judaism) required for a service.

⊂⊃ links

For more information about the Law in Judaism see Chapter 1, pages 18–19.

⊂⊃ links

Jewish boys and girls are believed to become adults after they have completed their Bar Mitzvah (boys) and Bat Mitzvah or Bat Chayil (girls). For more information about the Bar Mitzvah and Bat Chayil, see Chapter 5, pages 104–107.

A   A minimum of ten men are required for prayers in the Orthodox synagogue

Why ten adults?

The number required for the minyan was established in the Talmud, for example the interpretation of *Numbers* 14:27 where the word 'community' is used. It is only when the minimum number of ten Jews comes together for prayer that it is believed God is among them. It is believed that coming together in a group strengthens prayer and makes it more meaningful.

There is debate within Judaism as to why a minyan requires a minimum of ten adults but the number ten is important in Judaism. There are Ten Commandments, God sent ten plagues to Egypt, during the year there are ten days of repentance and Abraham was set ten tests. However, most scholars believe that the number ten required for the minyan originates from the need to make up to God for the lies told by ten of the 12 spies sent by Moses to find out about the land of Canaan. On their return these ten spies said that the land would be difficult to conquer as the people were big and strong, and the cities were well fortified. As a punishment for their lies, the Hebrews spent

Beliefs and teachings

How long will this wicked community grumble against me? I have heard the complaints of these grumbling Israelites.

Numbers 14:27

Beliefs and teachings

Boaz took ten of the elders of the town and said, 'sit here', and they did so.

Ruth 4:2

the next 40 years wandering in the desert and the people of the generation that left Egypt were to die out before they reached the Promised Land. An account of the ten spies' lies and God's punishment for their lies is found in the Torah: Numbers 13 and 14. The minyan is also referred to in Ruth 4:2.

The advantage of a minyan

The advantage of a minyan is that it means that when Jews do not have access to a synagogue they can still come together for acts of communal worship anywhere, so long as there is a minimum of ten adults present. However this can still be difficult if there is a very small Orthodox Jewish community, as ten adult males might be difficult to find. In the Nazi concentration camps, the minyan played an important role in enabling Jews to continue to worship, although this worship had to be in secret.

B   *Moses and the Ten Commandments*

Jewish worship in the Bergen-Belsen concentration camp

A survivor of the Bergen-Belsen concentration camp remembers: 'worship services held at night in the barracks, with people chanting the Sabbath or holiday literature while standing in the high and narrow canyons between the bunk beds; a hastily gathered minyan near one of the bunks saying Kaddish before a corpse was removed from the barracks.' (Thomas Rahe)

Case study

Activities

1. Explain what is meant by a minyan.
2. Explain the importance of the minyan for Jews.
3. Give one explanation for the choice of a minimum of ten adult Jews to form a minyan.
4. Why do you think a minyan is important to Jews living in small Jewish communities? Explain your opinion.
5. 'There should not be a set number of people for public worship to take place in synagogue.' Do you agree? Give reasons for your opinion showing that you have thought about more than one point of view.

Extension activity

Read Numbers 13 and 14 in the Torah or Old Testament. Write an account of the events that occurred when the ten spies lied to Moses.

Explain God's response to these lies.

∞ links

For information about the Kaddish prayer see page 45 of this chapter.

Summary

You should now be able to explain what is meant by a minyan in Judaism and its importance.

AQA   *Examiner's tip*

Learn the definition of a 'minyan' found in the key term box.

2.4 The synagogue

What is a synagogue?

Synagogue means 'bringing together' and is the name given to the Jewish place of worship. A synagogue can be anywhere and any shape and size, but the buildings are usually rectangular. Synagogues as places of worship date back to at least c. 560 BCE when the Jews were in exile in Babylonia.

Many Orthodox Jews call the synagogue 'shul'. 'Shul' means 'school' and this shows the importance of the synagogue as the place in which Jews learn more about their faith: as a place of education. The 'shul' is also the name of the library within the synagogue where Jews can go to study their religion. Many Reform Jews will often refer to a synagogue as a 'temple' because they believe their synagogue is a replacement for the Temple in Jerusalem destroyed in 70 BCE. However, Orthodox Jews would find it offensive to refer to a synagogue as a 'temple', believing that when the Messiah comes, the Temple in Jerusalem will be rebuilt.

The synagogue is usually run by a board of directors who are members of the community. In an Orthodox synagogue the board will be made up only of men but in a Reform synagogue there may be women directors. Another role in the synagogue taken by lay people is that of the Gabbai, whose role is to organise the Torah readings in the synagogue and to choose the people who will read from the Torah in the Shabbat services. The Gabbai needs to be skilled in reading Hebrew as they will stand next to the person reading the passages in the service to ensure that they pronounce the words correctly.

 A synagogue in Budapest, Hungary

Activities

1. Who runs a synagogue?
2. Explain why Orthodox Jews would not use the word 'temple' when referring to a synagogue.
3. Explain why Orthodox Jews will sometimes use the word 'shul' when referring to a synagogue.

The importance of the synagogue to the Jewish community

A synagogue is not only the place of public worship but also a community centre and a place of education. The activities other than worship that take place in synagogues include:

- classes in Hebrew for boys, and in the case of the Reform synagogues girls, who are preparing for their Bar or Bat Mitzvah
- discussion groups about aspects of the faith
- adult education classes
- kindergarten facilities for young children

Research activity

Using the internet and/or library, or by visiting a local synagogue, find out what further activities might take place in the synagogue besides worship or find some specific examples of the activities listed here.

Design a leaflet that could be given to members of the Jewish community to remind them of the events/activities at their synagogue with which they could be involved.

- youth clubs
- sporting activities such as football teams
- luncheon clubs and other gatherings for senior citizens
- music and drama groups
- celebration of festivals – such as community meals
- celebration of rites of passage such as a Bar Mitzvah or marriage ceremony
- charity events to raise money to support the work of organisations such as World Jewish Relief or to provide aid at the time of disaster
- providing social welfare for those in need in the community.

B   *The New London Synagogue*

Manchester Reform Synagogue

Case study

Manchester Reform Synagogue has members from all ages and the synagogue offers a wide range of activities that include:

- regular Shabbat and festival services (including family and children services)
- adult and multi-faith educational activities
- Cheder school for teaching for children from 5 to 13 the beliefs and teachings of Judaism
- conversion classes
- activities for people of all age ranges, from youth, through young adults, to older members
- shul visits for schools.

You can find out more about the activities of the synagogue on its website: **www.mcr-reform.org.uk/rabbi.htm**

AQA *Examiner's tip*

If you are asked to explain the importance of the synagogue to the Jewish community, don't forget to include both worship and the other activities.

Activities

4   Using the information on these pages, explain how the synagogue is important not only as a place of worship but also as a community centre.

5   'Synagogues should only be used for worship.' Do you agree? Give reasons for your opinion, showing that you have thought about more than one point of view.

Extension activity

Design a webpage for an Orthodox synagogue explaining all the activities that take place there.

Summary

You should now be able to explain what is meant by a synagogue in Judaism, and evaluate its use as a community centre.

The exterior features and symbols of the synagogue

Can a synagogue be identified by the external features?

There are no rules stating what a synagogue should look like on the outside but there are usually symbols associated with Judaism that make it recognisable. There may be a representation of a **menorah** (seven-branched candlestick) and/or the six-pointed **Star of David** (Magen David).

The menorah

Jews believe that God told Moses how a menorah was to be designed and that they were to be used in the places of worship. Some Jews believe that menorahs represent the burning bush through which God spoke to Moses, and instructed Moses to return to Egypt to lead the Hebrews out of slavery.

A menorah with nine branches is used during the festival of Hanukkah and is only lit at that time. The menorah in the Temple had seven branches to represent the seven days of the week and was lit every evening by the priests. The menorah in the synagogue will generally have six or eight branches instead of the Temple menorah's seven, because exact duplication of the Temple's ritual items is considered improper.

Objectives

Identify and explain the main external features of a synagogue and explain their significance.

Key terms

Menorah: a seven-branched candlestick.

The Star of David: a symbol of Judaism said to represent the shield of King David who ruled Israel in the 10th century BCE (Magen David).

A A symbol of a menorah on a synagogue door

Extension activity

Read Exodus 25:31–40. Do you think that the description in this passage matches the design of menorahs found in synagogues? Explain your opinion.

Beliefs and teachings

Make a lampstand of pure gold and hammer it out, base and shaft; its flowerlike cups, buds and blossoms shall be of one piece with it. Six branches are to extend from the sides of the lampstand – three on one side and three on the other. Three cups shaped like almond flowers with buds and blossoms are to be on one branch, three on the next branch, and the same for all six branches extending from the lampstand. And on the lampstand there are to be four cups shaped like almond flowers with buds and blossoms. One bud shall be under the first pair of branches extending from the lampstand, a second bud under the second pair, and a third bud under the third pair – six branches in all. The buds and branches shall all be of one piece with the lampstand, hammered out of pure gold. Then make its seven lamps and set them up on it so that they light the space in front of it. Its wick trimmers and trays are to be of pure gold. A talent of pure gold is to be used for the lampstand and all these accessories. See that you make them according to the pattern shown you on the mountain.

Exodus 25:31-40

B The Star of David over a synagogue door

The Star of David

King David is considered to be one of the greatest kings in the history of Judaism. The Star of David (Magen David) is supposed to represent King David's shield. The two triangles that make up the star are inseparable and some scholars suggest that this represents the fact the Jews cannot be separated from God. Other scholars have suggested that as the top of the star points up towards God and the bottom down towards earth, it shows that Jews are in constant struggle between the events in the world and seeking to achieve what God expects of them.

Stained glass windows

Synagogues often have stained glass windows, which consist of patterns or pictures in coloured glass, since they are not allowed to have representations of humans or animals as Jews believe that it would break the second commandment from God not to have any images of living things (see the Second Commandment in the Beliefs and Teachings box). The stained glass can add decoration to the synagogue without using human or animal representation. The symbols of the menorah and/or the Star of David are often found in stained glass windows.

C   *How could you identify this building as a synagogue?*

Discussion activity

Read the Second Commandment below, and as a whole class discuss your thoughts on whether or not it matters if there are pictures of people or animals in a synagogue. Give reasons for your opinion.

Beliefs and teachings

You shall have no other gods before me.

You shall not make for yourself an idol

in the form of anything in heaven above

or on the earth beneath or in the waters below.

You shall not bow down to them or worship them;

Exodus 20:3–5

Activities

1   Look at the building in Photo **C**. How would you be able to identify the building as a synagogue?

2   What is the name of the symbol you have used to identify the synagogue?

3   Explain what the symbol represents.

⚭links

Find out more about how Jews keep the Sabbath holy by reading Chapter 3, pages 54–57 and Chapter 4, pages 82–83.

AQA   *Examiner's tip*

Make sure that you are able to explain the meaning and importance of the symbols of the menorah and the Star of David for Jews.

Summary

You should now be able to identify the main external features of a synagogue and explain their significance.

The interior features and symbols of the synagogue

The prayer hall

There is no set shape for the prayer hall in a synagogue but it must be a suitable shape for the Shabbat (Sabbath) worship. The usual shape is rectangular, with the seats arranged on three sides facing inwards toward the **bimah** in the centre. The fourth side is the focal point of worship, the **Aron Hakodesh** (the Ark). The Holy Ark is on the side that faces towards Jerusalem. In the UK this would mean that the Ark is on the eastern wall of the synagogue.

There are no representations of figures, of the prophets for example, in the synagogue, because this would break the Second Commandment not to have idols. Decoration is therefore restricted to extracts from the scriptures or patterns and symbols.

In the prayer hall, there will be a seat for the rabbi and a pulpit from which the sermon can be given during Shabbat worship. The prayers are led by the cantor (a trained singer) so there will probably be a cantor's seat in the prayer hall.

The prayer hall is sometimes called the little 'sanctuary' because this links to the holy place in the Temple in Jerusalem. The sanctuary was the holiest part of the Temple and contained the holy place, which could only be entered by a priest twice a day. In the very centre was the Holy of Holies, a small windowless room in which God was believed to be present. Some Orthodox Jews would not agree with comparing synagogues with the Temple in this kind of way as they believe that only the Messiah can rebuild the Temple when he returns. This Third Temple will be on the site of the other two Temples.

Aron Hakodesh

The Aron Hakodesh (the Holy Ark) is the most important feature in the prayer hall because it is where the Torah is kept. The Aron Hakodesh is set in the wall facing Jerusalem where the Temple stood. The Ark is usually raised above steps as a reminder that God is above his people and they must 'go up' to the Torah because it is higher than humanity.

The Holy Ark represents the Holy of Holies in the Temple that contained the Ark of the Covenant, which held the Ten Commandments in Moses' time. Above the Ark there are usually two stone tablets on which the first two words of each of the Ten Commandments are written in Hebrew as a further reminder of the link between the Aron Hakodesh and the Ten Commandments given by God to Moses. The Aron Hakodesh is where the handwritten parchment scrolls of the Torah are kept when not in use during worship. The Holy Ark is a cupboard with either doors or curtains that are only opened to take out the relevant scroll (Sefer Torah) during worship.

Objectives

Identify the main internal features of a synagogue and explain their significance.

Key terms

Bimah: a platform in a synagogue from which the Torah is read.

Aron Hakodesh: the Ark – part of the synagogue containing Torah scrolls.

Ner Tamid: a light kept burning in the synagogue – continual light.

links

Remind yourself of the decoration used in a synagogue by rereading pages 38–39 of this chapter.

Remind yourself of why men and women sit separately in Orthodox synagogues by rereading page 31 of this chapter.

links

There is more information about the roles of the rabbi and cantor on pages 48–49 of this chapter.

A *The Aron Hakodesh in a synagogue, showing the ner tamid*

Ner tamid

The **ner tamid** (eternal light) is kept burning at all times in front of the Ark as a reminder that God is eternal. It is a reminder of the seven-branched candlestick (menorah) that was always kept burning in the Temple. There may also be a menorah nearby.

The bimah

In the centre of the synagogue there will be the bimah, a raised platform from which the rabbi leads the service and from which the Torah is read. Some Jews believe that the bimah is a reminder of the altar that was a central feature of the courtyard of the Temple. It was also the place from which the Torah was read and the priest would address the people. The bimah is usually placed in the centre of the synagogue. Once the relevant scrolls for the service have been removed from the Aron Hakodesh and taken to the bimah, this raised platform becomes the focus of worship.

B *The prayer hall in a synagogue*

∞ links

For more information about the Torah and its importance, see Chapter 1, pages 8–9 and 24–25.

Extension activity

The scrolls are 'dressed' in symbolic objects that link back to the robes of the Temple priests in Jerusalem. Using the internet and/or library find out what the following features on the scroll of the Torah represent: a breast-plate, bells and the mantle.

Activities

1. Describe how the Aron Hakodesh (the Ark) and the bimah are used in a synagogue.
2. Explain why the ner tamid is kept burning at all times.
3. Explain how features in the prayer hall are reminders of Temple worship in Jerusalem.
4. 'Jews should be looking to the future and not to the past in the design of their synagogues.' Do you agree? Give reasons for your answer showing that you have thought about more than one point of view.

AQA Examiner's tip

In your examination you might be given a colour picture or a plan of a synagogue to use as a starting point for your answer. So make sure that you can recognise the main features of a synagogue; they are also important for understanding worship.

Summary

You should now be able to describe the interior features of the synagogue in Judaism and to explain the function and symbolism of the main features of the synagogue.

Orthodox and Reform synagogues

A   *Prayer hall in an Orthodox synagogue*

Objectives

Understand how the different attitudes to worship in the Orthodox and Reform traditions reflect and affect the design of the synagogue.

Orthodox and Reform synagogues

The main features of the Aron Hakodesh (the Holy Ark), the bimah (reading platform) and ner tamid (ever-burning light) are found in both Orthodox and Reform synagogues because both traditions regard these as important to the acts of worship. However there are differences between the design of the Orthodox and Reform synagogues. This is because Orthodox Jews believe that no changes should be made from the teaching in the Torah and the teaching of the Torah has influenced the accepted design of the synagogue, whereas Reform Jews allow changes to occur that match the changing world around them.

Some of the activities other than worship that take place in Orthodox and Reform synagogues may be social events and therefore there is usually a kosher kitchen as part of the synagogue facilities, as well as a library and a function hall.

An Orthodox synagogue

One important difference between an Orthodox and a Reform synagogue is that men and women sit separately in an Orthodox synagogue. As women are not allowed to sit with the men during the services in an Orthodox synagogue or to take a role in the services, there will be a separate area of seating for the women and boys under 13 years of age. This seating is often a balcony above the prayer hall so that the women and young boys can see and hear the services but are separate from the men. This separate section is a reminder of the women's courtyard in the Temple. Women were not allowed to go beyond this point in the Temple. Married women will cover their heads in an Orthodox synagogue.

links

Remind yourself of the activities other than worship that take place in synagogues by re-reading pages 36–37 of this chapter.

links

Find out more about kosher food in Judaism by reading Chapter 4, pages 76–77.

links

Remind yourself of why women sit separately from the men in Orthodox synagogues by re-reading page 31 of this chapter.

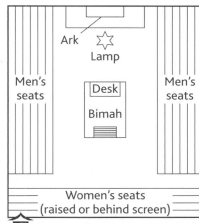

C   *An example of the layout of an Orthodox synagogue*

B   *Men and women worship together in a Reform synagogue*

A Reform synagogue

In a Reform synagogue men and women sit together along with the children. Men and women are allowed to take equal roles in the service; therefore there is no need for a separate section for the women and boys under 13. It is a matter of personal choice as to whether women cover their heads in a Reform synagogue.

The bimah is usually placed in the centre of the Reform synagogue as in an Orthodox synagogue, but sometimes it is placed in front of the Ark so that the focus can be on both features during the service.

In an Orthodox synagogue only the human voice is used to praise God as it is believed that it is forbidden to use musical instruments, especially during Shabbat worship. In a Reform synagogue there may be an organ to accompany the singing. Some Reform synagogues use a microphone during the services but microphones are never used in an Orthodox synagogue.

The community of Reform Jews will decide for themselves how they want their synagogue to be decorated.

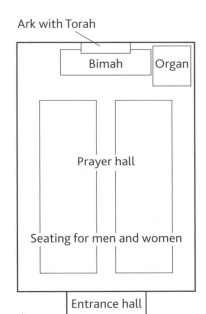

D   *An example of the layout of a reform synagogue*

Activities

1   What features are common to all synagogues?

2   Explain one feature in an Orthodox synagogue that will not be found in a Reform synagogue.

3   Explain why Orthodox Jews believe that they should not change the design of the synagogue.

4   'All synagogues should have the same features.' What do you think? Explain your opinion.

Summary

You should now be able to recognise some of the different features found in Orthodox and Reform synagogues.

AQA   Examiner's tip

Make sure that you are able to explain how synagogues reflect and affect the style of worship that takes place within them.

Why is Shabbat worship important?

The most important form of worship that takes place in the synagogue is Shabbat (Sabbath) worship. Jews believe that God has instructed them in the Fourth Commandment to observe the Sabbath and to keep it holy. Jews believe that keeping the Sabbath holy includes worship in the home and in the synagogue. The Jewish Sabbath begins at dusk on Friday evening and ends at dusk on Saturday evening. In the Genesis account, God's creation took six days and then God rested on the seventh day of the week. The Shabbat is the seventh day of the week and therefore is to be kept as a day of rest as instructed in the Fourth Commandment.

Shabbat worship

The whole family attends the Saturday morning service in the synagogue. The men wear prayer shawls and cover their heads before the service begins. The service lasts for about two hours. The first part of the service follows the same format as other daily services of prayers and psalms.

> Our God and God of our Ancestors!
> Be pleased with our rest; sanctify us
> with Your commandments, give us a
> share in Your Torah, satiate us with
> Your bounty, and gladden us in Your salvation.
> Cleanse our hearts to serve You in truth: let us inherit,
> O Lord our God, in love and favour Your holy Sabbath,
> and may Israel, who loves Your name, rest thereon.
> Praised are You, O Lord, who sanctifies the Sabbath.
>
> *Extract from the Shabbat Amidah*

The Amidah or 'standing prayer' is then offered by the congregation in silence as they stand facing the Aron Hakodesh, which means that they are also facing Jerusalem. As they pray, Jews are expected to clear their minds of everyday concerns and to concentrate on God and the blessings that they have received from God. Jews can insert their own prayers into the Amidah but must not ask for anything for themselves on the Sabbath. The Amidah is shorter during Sabbath worship than when it is used in daily worship.

After the Amidah, two members of the congregation go to the Aron Hakodesh (the Holy Ark) and take out the scroll that is to be used for the reading from the Torah. In the course of a year the whole Torah, from Genesis to Deuteronomy, is read during Shabbat services. As soon as the last passage from Deuteronomy has been read, then the beginning of Genesis is read and the cycle of readings begins again. This is to show that the message of the Torah is eternal. It is a great honour to be chosen to read from the Torah. After the Torah scroll is removed from the Aron Hakodesh, the congregation say the Shema: this is the Jewish statement of belief. The scroll is carried around the

Objectives

Know and understand the main features and importance of Shabbat worship in the synagogue.

links

For more information about Shabbat and its importance, including the definition of the term, see Chapter 3, pages 54–57 and Chapter 4, pages 82–83.

links

For the Fourth Commandment instructing Jews to keep the Sabbath holy, see Chapter 3, page 54.

A *The Torah scroll is removed from the Aron Hakodesh during the service*

links

For more information about the prayer shawls (tallit) worn by men for worship read page 32 of this chapter.

links

For more information about daily worship read pages 46–47 of this chapter.

synagogue in procession to the bimah. The congregation bow as the scroll passes and if close enough they will touch or kiss the Torah and then kiss the hand that touched it.

Beliefs and teachings

(The Shabbat service)

May his great name grow exalted and sanctified,
in the world that he created as he willed. May he make his kingship reign in your lifetimes and in your days, and in the lifetimes of all the Jewish people, swiftly and soon; now respond: Amen.
May his great name be blessed forever and ever.
Blessed, praised, glorified, exalted, extolled,
mighty, upraised, and lauded be the name of the Holy One, Blessed is he beyond any blessing and song,
praise and consolation that are uttered in the world. Now respond: Amen.
May there be great peace from Heaven,
and life upon us and upon all Israel; now respond: Amen.
He who makes peace in his Heavens, may he make peace upon us and upon all Israel.

Kaddish prayer

As the section from the Torah is chanted in Hebrew, the words are followed by a pointer made of wood or silver called a yad. This is out of respect for the word of God and Jews try to avoid touching the Torah scrolls unless absolutely necessary. After the reading has ended, the scroll is returned to the Aron Hakodesh.

The rabbi will then deliver a sermon to the congregation and even in Orthodox synagogues this will be in the language of the congregation. It will explain the meaning of the passage of the Torah that was read and how to put God's laws into practice. The rabbi will explain to the congregation how to live their lives as God would wish, according to the Jewish teachings and beliefs.

The service will end with prayers, including the Aleinu prayer that reminds the congregation of the Jewish struggle to obey God. The prayer of sanctification, the Kaddish, follows. This prayer is said at funerals and those in the congregation who have died are often remembered at this point. Kaddish means 'holy' and is so called because it begins by stating the holiness of God. The Kaddish is a prayer of blessing that is frequently said for the souls of the dead at funerals. The prayer praises God and acknowledges that God knows best. There will be prayers for the country in which they live, prayers for the ruler of the country and for the State of Israel. The service ends with singing of a famous Jewish hymn Adon Olam (Master of the World) that praises God.

Activities

1. Describe the main features of Shabbat worship.
2. Explain the importance of Shabbat worship in the synagogue.
3. Explain why the Torah scrolls are treated with such respect.
4. 'The sermon should be in Hebrew as this is the language of the Torah.' Do you agree? Give reasons for your answer showing that you have thought about more than one point of view.

Discussion activity

With a partner, in a group or as a whole class, discuss why you think that Jews are not allowed to ask for anything for themselves during the Shabbat prayers. Give reasons for your opinion.

B *The Torah scrolls are read using a yad (pointer)*

links

If you are not sure of the function of the Aron Hakodesh and bimah re-read pages 40–41 of this chapter.

AQA Examiner's tip

Make sure that you are able to use the key terms associated with Shabbat worship correctly.

Research activity

Find out what is said in the Adon Olam prayer by looking it up on the website: **www.hebrewsongs. com**

Write an explanation of what this prayer is teaching about the Jewish beliefs about God and the Jews' relationship with God.

Summary

You should now be able to describe and explain the main features of Shabbat worship in the synagogue.

Daily prayers

Daily prayers in the synagogue, with a minyan, are believed to strengthen prayer but it may not be possible for Jews to attend the daily services in the synagogue. Therefore they can recite the three daily prayers anywhere that is acceptable. If a Jew is travelling, it may be necessary to say the prayers wherever they are at the time. If Jews are praying alone, they cannot recite the Kiddush prayer as this prayer, or any prayers associated with the reading of the Torah, are never said without a minyan.

Jews are expected to pray three times a day: in the morning (Shacharit), afternoon (Mincha) and evening (Ma'ariv). There are usually three daily prayer services in the synagogue to coincide with these times of daily prayer. Prayer at regular times during the day is important because it means that God is kept within an individual's thoughts throughout the day. Orthodox Jews and many Reform Jews say the daily prayers in Hebrew.

Prayers are said standing, as this is a reminder that Jews are in the presence of God. The prayers are said silently when praying alone or quietly in the synagogue. This is because God is believed to know what is in the person's heart and therefore it is not necessary to say them loudly. The length of the prayers said may vary from day to day or according to the festivals or holy days as certain prayers are added or omitted according to the day of the week or time of year. The daily prayers are collected together in a book called the *Siddur*. This is a Hebrew word meaning order and the book shows the order of the daily prayers.

Additional services may be added during festivals and holy days. Scholars believe that there are three main daily services as this is the number of sacrifices that were held each day in the Temple in Jerusalem. Central to all prayers in Judaism are the beliefs expressed in the Shema.

Research activity

Using the internet and/or library, research the worship in Herod's Temple in Jerusalem that was destroyed in 70 CE.

Write an account of the form the worship took in the Temple.

Morning prayers

The tallit and tefillin are worn for the morning prayers as these are considered to be the most important prayers of the day. Tefillin are not worn on Shabbat and festivals. Morning prayer is the most important daily prayer because as Jews wake they can say thank you to God for giving them another day. This is why the prayers begin with the words: 'I give thanks to You, living and eternal King, for having restored within me my soul with mercy; great is Your trust.'

Objectives

Know and understand the features and importance of daily prayer in Judaism.

Evaluate the importance of prayer in Judaism.

links

For more information about the minyan read pages 34–35 of this chapter.

Extension activity

Using the internet find out more about the daily prayers on the website:
www.jewfaq.org

Write a detailed description of daily prayer in Judaism.

Discussion activity

As a whole class read the extract from the Shema found on page 45 of this chapter.

Based on these words from the Shema discuss the reasons why prayer is an important part of the Jewish day.

A *Prayers are said standing*

Verses of praise and passages from the Psalms follow as well as the words recorded in Exodus when the Red Sea was parted to allow the Israelites to escape from Egypt. The Shema is then recited and the Amidah. The Amidah during daily prayer is longer than the version said during the Shabbat service as it contains reference to the 18 blessings from God. At this point Jews will lower their heads in supplication to God, and humbly ask God for his forgiveness for sins they have committed. A Torah reading will follow and additional prayers, ending with the closing Aleinu prayer, which is a reminder of the struggles and responsibilities Jews have to accept as God's chosen people and the need of faith and dedication to the eternal God.

∞links

For more information about the tallit and tefillin worn for worship read pages 32–33 of this chapter.

B   *Jews wear the tallit and tefillin for morning prayer*

Afternoon prayers

Only the tallit is worn for the afternoon prayers. The service consists mainly of prayers but on the Shabbat and fast days the Torah is read. Psalm 145 is always said during afternoon prayers. The prayers end with the Aleinu prayer.

Evening prayers

As with the afternoon prayers only the tallit is worn for evening prayers. In the evening prayers the Shema, Amidah and the Aleinu prayers are said.

C   *A Jew may pray anywhere*

Activities

1   Describe morning prayers in Judaism.

2   Explain why daily prayer is important in Judaism.

3   'The tefillin should be worn for all prayers.' What do you think? Explain your opinion.

4   'A Jew can pray when they want to and don't need set times.' What do you think? Explain your opinion.

Summary

You should now be able to describe and explain the main features and importance of daily prayer in Judaism.

AQA   *Examiner's tip*

You do not need to know the Hebrew words used in this book unless they are key terms. However, it may be interesting to know what they are.

The rabbi

The **rabbi** is the leader of the services in the synagogue and a teacher of all aspects of Jewish law including the Torah, Talmud and Halakhah. In Orthodox synagogues the rabbi is always a man, but in Reform synagogues the rabbi may be a woman. The rabbi will lead the worship in the synagogue. The rabbi will also conduct weddings and funerals. This will include explaining to the bride and groom the meaning of the words that they are saying in the wedding ceremony and the importance of marriage in Judaism. As well as conducting a funeral, another role is to comfort the family who has lost a loved one. The rabbi will also visit the sick in the community, including those in hospital. The rabbi, as the leader of the synagogue, is usually the synagogue's representative in the wider community. This may include taking part in interfaith dialogues with other religions.

Rabbis undergo extensive training so that they are able to teach the meaning of the Torah and Talmud to the congregation, and explain how to live according to this teaching. A rabbi will usually have trained at a Jewish college for a number of years. Rabbis not only read from the Torah in the services but, in the sermon, also explain the meaning of the passages read. Another role for a rabbi is as a teacher whose task it is to educate the community about all aspects of the faith. This may include teaching Hebrew to those who are preparing for their Bar/Bat Mitzvah.

There is no specific dress for a rabbi other than that expected of other Jews. Rabbis can marry and have a normal family life. In fact this is encouraged, as the experience of marriage and bringing up a family will bring greater understanding of issues that face members of the congregation, as it is to the rabbi that they will often turn for advice.

Objectives

Know and understand the role of the rabbi and chazzan in Judaism.

Key terms

Rabbi: A religious leader and teacher.

Chazzan (cantor): a person who leads or chants prayers in the synagogue.

⊂⊃links

For more information about Halakhah read Chapter 1, pages 12–13.

⊂⊃links

For more information about Bar and Bat Mitzvah read Chapter 5, pages 104–107.

A A rabbi preaching in a synagogue

B *Rabbis often prepare teenagers for their Bar/Bat Mitzvah*

Extension activity

Find out more about the role of the Chazzan at www.askmoses.com and make a report of your findings.

Research activity

Using the internet and/or library find out more about the training and role of the chazzan.

Write an explanation of the training of the chazzan and why this role is important.

A day in the life of a Rabbi

Case study

Every day is different for a rabbi as they can never know when they may be needed to help someone with a problem or attend a person who is dying. Most rabbis will begin the day by studying the Torah before they lead the morning prayers at the synagogue. After breakfast there may be a wedding or funeral to arrange or even perform, and then a visit to someone who is sick or depressed may occur. In the afternoon, there may be a meeting with the leaders of the synagogue to discuss matters related to the synagogue or a visit to the local hospital or school. There will be evening prayers to be said and at some point the sermon for the Shabbat service needs to be written. At least once a week the rabbi will be involved in classes for those taking their Bar Mitzvah and others who are planning to convert to Judaism. The rabbi will also be involved in the social life of the synagogue.

The chazzan

The **chazzan** in Judaism is the cantor, a trained singer. The purpose of the chazzan is to lead the worshippers in their singing or, to be more accurate, chanting. This is necessary in Orthodox synagogues as musical instruments are not used, but a cantor will also lead the singing in a Reform synagogue where an organ may be used. All that is required to become a cantor is that the person is of good moral character and has knowledge of the prayers and chants used in worship. They will have training to lead the singing.

The chazzan will chant parts of the prayers during Shabbat worship and other festivals as well as at weddings and funeral services. They will help young people who are preparing to go through their Bar/Bat Mitzvah to learn how to chant the passages that they are to read in the ceremony.

Activities

1 Explain the role of the rabbi in Judaism.

2 Explain the role of the chazzan in Judaism.

3 'If God created everyone to be equal, then a rabbi or chazzan should not have to be a man.' Do you agree? Give reasons for your opinion showing that you have thought about more than one point of view.

Summary

You should now know and understand the importance of the role of the rabbi and cantor in Judaism.

AQA Examiner's tip

Make sure that you are able to explain the roles of the rabbi and chazzan in the examination.

2

The synagogue and worship – summary

For the examination you should know and understand:

- how the synagogue reflects and affects the style of worship that takes place in it
- the design and function of synagogues
- features and symbols in the synagogue, including: bimah, Aron Hakodesh, Ner Tamid, menorah and the Star of David and the importance of these features
- daily prayer
- tallit and tefillin
- the minyan
- the leaders of the community with special reference to the rabbi and chazzan (cantor)
- Discuss the importance of worship and places of worship from different points of view, including Jewish ones.

Sample answer

1   Write an answer to the following exam question:

'Prayers in the synagogue are more important than prayers said at home.'

What do you think? Explain your opinion.   *(3 marks)*

2   Read the following sample answer:

> I agree that one should be able to pray anywhere because I believe that God is everywhere and can hear our prayers. I think that prayer is between an individual and God and so can be said at home.

3   With a partner discuss the sample answer. Do you think that there are other things that the student could have included in the answer?

4   What mark would you give this answer out of three? Look at the mark scheme in the Introduction on page 7 (AO2). What are the reasons for the mark you have given?

AQA Examination-style questions

1   Look at the photograph below and answer the following questions.

(a)   Explain the importance of the symbol in the picture for Jews.   *(2 marks)*

(b)   Explain the importance of the main internal features of a synagogue.   *(6 marks)*

(c)   'It is important to wear the tefillin for morning prayers.' Do you agree? Give reasons for your answer showing you have thought about more than one point of view.   *(6 marks)*

(d)   Explain why synagogues are important to Jewish communities.   *(6 marks)*

 Examiner's tip   Remember when you are asked 'Do you agree' with a statement, you must show what you think and the reasons why other people might take a different view. If your answer is one sided, you can only achieve a maximum of four marks. If you make no comment about religious belief or practice, you will achieve no more than three marks.

3.1 Festivals

Celebration and commemoration

> 66 *There is a time for everything, and a season for every activity under heaven: ...*
>
> *a time to weep and a time to laugh,*
>
> *a time to mourn and a time to dance,*
>
> *a time to scatter stones and a time to gather them,*
>
> *a time to embrace and a time to refrain.* 99
>
> *Ecclesiastes 3:1, 4–5*

These verses from Ecclesiastes in the Ketuvim sum up the Jewish attitudes to **festivals** very well. There are times for happiness (celebration) and sadness (commemoration). Some festivals have a mixture of celebration and commemoration. The festival of Pesach commemorates (remembers) bad times for the Hebrews when they were slaves in Egypt but it also celebrates the freedom they gained once they had left Egypt.

Festivals occur at set times within the Jewish calendar, ranging from Rosh Hashanah (New Year) in September and Hanukkah in December to Pesach in April. These dates do fluctuate a little because the Jewish calendar differs from the Gregorian calendar, which is the internationally accepted calendar used in Britain.

A Hannukah is a time of celebration and happiness

Key terms

Festival: a religious celebration or commemoration.

Research activity O⟍

Read the whole of the passage from Ecclesiastes 3:1–8.

This passage was rewritten as a popular song in 1959 by Pete Seeger. The most successful recording of it was the version by the Byrds in 1965. Try to listen to this version.

∞ links

For more about Pesach, see 3.6 and 3.7 on pages 62–65.

AQA *Examiner's tip*

In your exam, try to use the word 'celebrate' for happy festivals and 'commemorate' for sad ones.

Activity

1 Explain the difference between celebration and commemoration.

■ The historical basis for festivals

Most festivals in Judaism, for example Pesach, are rooted in the past. They remember with joy or sadness, or both, an event of great significance in Jewish history. This may be ancient history from more than 3,000 years ago; on the other hand, Holocaust Remembrance day commemorates the death of six million Jews during the Second World War between 1939 and 1945. The joyful events usually celebrate God's intervention on their behalf, often involving him working miracles for them. These show the Jews that God has been willing to influence events and human affairs according to his plan. Celebrating such events, even those that took place 3,000 years ago, shows gratitude to God for his intervention. Those that are not joyful have caused Jews to question the actions of their forefathers that may have prevented God intervening to save them, in the hope that they can learn valuable lessons for the future.

Other festivals focus either on God the creator and sustainer of the universe (e.g. Shabbat) or on the relationship individual Jews have with their God (e.g. Yom Kippur).

■ Community focus of festivals

Festivals are either celebrated by Jews in their home or in the synagogue. Many of them include elements of both. The idea that Judaism is a community religion is shown by the fact that religious observance is based on both the community of the home and family and on the wider Jewish community based on the synagogue. Fellowship with other Jewish people is important because it helps them to sustain each other's faith, often in a wider community that may be hostile to Judaism and possibly to religion in general. It is common in most festivals to have a special family meal, which possibly includes some symbolic foods, although Yom Kippur, for example, is commemorated by fasting.

■ Tradition

As with much of Judaism, if Jews are asked why they do some of the things they do, the answer 'because it is the way we have always done it' is often given, especially from the Orthodox section of the faith. They see no need to change the way they celebrate festivals from the way their forefathers celebrated them hundreds of years ago. For many Jews, tradition is important and keeping festivals in the way they have always been kept is a way of sharing in a faith that has remained true to its origins and history. Reform Jews may adapt some of their practices to suit more modern times but the meaning behind the festival remains unchanged. This meaning is often seen in the symbolic nature of the celebration or commemoration, which all Jews are taught and which helps their understanding of their faith.

■ Conclusion

All these concepts and practices help to ensure that these festivals are regular features in Jewish life wherever in the world they live. This helps them to establish their identity and give them some consistency in an ever-changing world.

Discussion activity 👤👤👤

Using your previous study of Judaism, discuss with a partner which event in Jewish history you think should be marked by having a festival. How would you celebrate or commemorate this festival? Make this into a short presentation for the rest of the class.

Activities

2 Why do you think Jews involve both the family and the synagogue community in their festivals?

3 'Nobody should celebrate a festival on their own.' What do you think? Explain your opinion.

B *Festivals help Jews throughout the world to become united*

Activities

4 Explain the main difference between Orthodox and Reform Jews on their ideas about how festivals should be celebrated.

5 Give as many reasons as you can why Jews celebrate or commemorate festivals.

Summary

You should now understand more about Jewish festivals and practices associated with them and have thought about their place in Judaism.

3.2   Shabbat – origins and purpose

Shabbat – origins

Shabbat is a weekly festival that Jews observe. It begins at sunset on Friday (which for the Jews is the beginning of the new day) and lasts until sunset on Saturday. For Jews, this is the seventh day of the week. Shabbat is often referred to as Sabbath, which is a term that has become attached to Sunday in the Christian tradition. Although Sabbath is an acceptable way to refer to Shabbat, there are major differences between Jewish Shabbat and the Christian Sabbath.

Jews regard Shabbat as a day of complete rest set aside to worship and focus on God. They believe that it is a requirement of their faith and has its origins in the story of creation:

Beliefs and teachings

Thus the heavens and the earth were completed in all their vast array. By the seventh day God had finished the work he had been doing; so on the seventh day he rested from all his work. And God blessed the seventh day and made it holy, because on it he rested from all the work of creating he had done.

Genesis 2:1–3

The idea that Jews should follow the example of God in resting on the seventh day became formalised as a required Jewish practice by its inclusion in the Ten Commandments:

Beliefs and teachings

Remember the Sabbath day by keeping it holy. Six days you shall labour and do all your work, but the seventh day is a Sabbath to the Lord your God. On it you shall not do any work … For in six days the Lord made the heavens and the earth, the sea and all that is in them, but he rested on the seventh day. Therefore the Lord blessed the seventh day and made it holy.

Exodus 20:8–11

Thus in observing Shabbat, Jews are obeying the commandment but also imitating the example of God. He created the Earth for all people (or everyone) and expects his people to follow his example by having a day off work every week, just as he did.

Shabbat is also an important opportunity for families to spend time resting and focusing on God together and also allows them to join the synagogue congregation in communal worship without work getting in the way. There are services in the synagogue as Shabbat starts, on Saturday morning and as Shabbat finishes.

A *Jews believe that God created the world*

Preparations for Shabbat

Because no work can be done on Shabbat, preparations have to be made the day before (Friday before sunset). Therefore, usually the wife and mother of the family will spend much of Friday preparing and cooking food for Shabbat. This will include the special Friday night Shabbat meal for which she will have to bake or buy the special challah bread that is a feature of the religious observance before the main evening meal. Meals for the next day are also prepared and are either allowed to keep warm or more likely eaten cold. The house is cleaned, with the children helping out once they get back home from school. In this way, they learn more about Shabbat observance and the requirements it makes upon them now and when they have their own home. Once everything is ready, everybody washes or bathes and changes into clean, smart clothes for the beginning of the most important day of the week. Shabbat is often thought of as a special guest who visits every week so everything has to be done well.

The table for the Shabbat meal is set with the best cutlery and crockery before sunset, with special Shabbat candles that are lit just before the beginning of Shabbat to welcome Shabbat into the house. It would be forbidden to light them once Shabbat has begun, because making fire is classed as work and therefore not allowed on the day of rest.

links

For information on Shabbat laws regarding work, see 4.5.

Lighting the Shabbat candles to start Shabbat is an important part of my role and duty as a wife and mother. I know that thousands of women in Britain are doing the same thing at this time.

C *Shabbat is about to start*

Summary

You should now know about the origins of Shabbat and have evaluated the idea of having a special day to rest and focus on God.

3.3 Shabbat celebrations

The Friday night Shabbat observance

The Friday night observance starts with a strong religious focus before later becoming similar to any other special meal, apart from the fact that it is all prepared and cooked before sunset. Once the candles are lit between 15 and 20 minutes before sunset, the wife and mother welcomes in the Shabbat by beckoning with her arms, moving them around the candles and covering her eyes to recite a blessing.

Beliefs and teachings

Blessed are you, Lord our God, King of the universe, who has sanctified us by His commandments, and has commanded us to kindle the light of the holy Shabbat.

studentorgs.utexas.edu/cjso/Shabbos/Brochos.html

She also says a short prayer asking God to support the family. A family may attend a special Shabbat service at the synagogue. This is a service that includes the welcoming in of Shabbat and the recitation of psalms and is often joyful, with children being involved in providing music.

At home, the meal starts with the husband and father blessing the children in the hope that they will continue the faith and observance with their own children in the future. He will then recite Kiddush blessings, including sharing red wine, with the others saying Amen at the end of each blessing.

They then all wash their hands as an act of purification before retaking their places at the table. The man leading the ceremony blesses the challah bread, thanking God for providing them with food. He then cuts the challah bread and dips pieces in salt before passing them round. They are dipped in salt as a reminder of sacrifices being dipped in salt before being offered in the Temple. The actual meal follows. It can take several hours, with stories being told and songs being sung between courses. Enjoying the company of their family, and possibly friends whom they may invite, is worth spending time over.

B *A Jewish family celebrates Shabbat*

Objectives

Know and understand how Jews celebrate Shabbat.

⚭ links

For more about Kiddush blessings, see 2.8.

A *The scroll is read in the synagogue on Shabbat*

Activities

1. Describe what happens during Friday night Shabbat observance.

2. Why do you think it is the woman who welcomes the Shabbat into the home?

3. Remembering that no work is to be done on Shabbat, what are the advantages to Jewish families and friends of spending several hours over a meal on a Friday evening?

The Saturday morning service

Jews are encouraged to visit the synagogue on Saturday morning, although they should be careful to restrict travelling to just sufficient to get to the synagogue and back. Most Jews ensure they live close to a synagogue so this is not a problem. The service is a little longer than a weekday morning service, consisting of prayers, blessings, processing and then reading the Torah and a sermon preached by the rabbi or maybe a visiting speaker. As people leave the service they wish each other 'Shabbat Shalom', which literally means 'Have a peaceful Shabbat'.

Havdalah, the end of Shabbat

Some Jews also attend synagogue for the end of Shabbat. In addition to the features of the normal weekday evening service, this service includes a prayer asking God to bless the community/congregation throughout the coming week and finishes with the rabbi performing havdalah. This involves him making four blessings, the first over a glass of wine and the second over a box of fragrant spices, usually cloves, cinnamon or bay leaves. This symbolises the hope that the coming week will be good (fragrant). The third is made over a special havdalah candle (see Photo **B**), which is lit to show that Shabbat is over and fire can once more be made. The final blessing is the actual havdalah blessing made over wine, much of which is then drunk. Once the blessing has been said, the candle is extinguished in the remaining wine. The final blessing is as follows:

> 66 *Blessed are you, Lord, our God, sovereign of the universe who separates between sacred and secular between light and darkness, between Israel and the nations between the seventh day and the six days of labour. Blessed are You, Lord, who separates between sacred and secular. (Amen)* 99

The blessings are also performed in the home, usually led by the father. The spices, wine and havdalah candle feature in these blessings as in the synagogue.

CO links

For more on Shabbat worship see 2.8 pages 44–45.

AQA   *Examiner's tip*

There are differences between Orthodox and Reform worship. If you are writing about the Shabbat service, you can focus on just one denomination. To get full marks, you will need to provide good detail.

C   *The havdalah candle is lit when three stars can be seen in the sky to show Shabbat has ended*

Activities

4   Explain how Jews mark the end of Shabbat.
5   What is the symbolic significance of the spices and candle?
6   How do you think a Jewish person feels once Shabbat is over?

Discussion activity 👥👥👥

If you were involved in deciding how a day of rest and focus on God would be spent, what would you decide to do? Discuss this with a partner and give your reasons why.

Summary

You should now know and understand about Shabbat celebrations.

Extension activity

Analyse what the havdalah blessing means. Try to relate it to the meaning of Shabbat.

3.4 Rosh Hashanah

Days of Awe

Rosh Hashanah, and Yom Kippur which follows it, are often referred to as 'Days of Awe'. They are seen as two stages in the process of judgement and atonement. Atonement means to restore a relationship with God by trying to put right wrongs against God and individual people. Rosh Hashanah is the New Year festival starting on the 1st Tishri, which follows the month of Ellul – a month that Jews use to prepare themselves for judgement by making up for things they have done wrong throughout the year and preparing to renew their promises to God for the new year. Rosh Hashanah lasts for two days (1st and 2nd Tishri) and Yom Kippur starts with preparation on 9th Tishri before the festival itself next day.

Origins of Rosh Hashanah

Rosh Hashanah literally means 'head of the year' because it is the first day of the year. As with most Jewish festivals, Rosh Hashanah remembers a story from the Tenakh. In the case of Rosh Hashanah, this story is the creation story from the beginning of the book of Genesis. It is considered the anniversary of the day on which God created the first humans. It is believed that every year on this day, God writes down a person's bad deeds, judges them and makes decisions about what will be their fortune over the coming year.

A *The shofar is blown to announce the coming of the festival and also on the festival itself*

Celebrations of Rosh Hashanah

The month of Ellul before Rosh Hashanah is used by Jews to prepare for judgement. Every morning (except Shabbat) the shofar (ram's horn) is played in the synagogue to announce the coming of Rosh Hashanah – the day of judgement. During the month, special prayers asking for forgiveness are said. These are called selichot. On the final day of Ellul, the day before Rosh Hashanah, special selichot are recited, but to draw a distinction between the final day of preparation and the festival itself, the shofar is not blown.

Discussion activity

With a partner, spend five minutes discussing what a person can do to put right wrongs they have committed. Make a list and be prepared to share your ideas with others.

Activities

1 Why do you think Jews believe atonement is so important?

2 Write down your thoughts about the idea that God judges people every year and decides what their fortune will be over the coming year.

B *Greetings cards are given at Rosh Hashanah*

Rosh Hashanah starts at the sunset that ends the final day of Ellul (every Jewish day starts at sunset). No work is done, so preparations are made in a similar way to those made for Shabbat. Candles are lit just before the festival begins. As preparation, in addition to buying what is needed for a meal, the wife and mother buys fruit, including a variety of fruit they have not eaten for some time. This symbolises renewal, which is linked to judgement and atonement. They are eaten on the second day of the festival.

The evening synagogue service to mark the beginning of the festival starts with the usual evening service including the Kiddush blessing over wine. God is referred to as a king sitting in judgement over the world He created and the theme of the prayers is focused on asking God to accept the kingship of the world for the coming year. The usual greeting on leaving the synagogue is "L'shanah tovah" ('For a good year').

Once back home, Kiddush is recited and slices of apple dipped in honey are eaten. These symbolise the hope for a sweet new year. A fish head may also be eaten to symbolise the wish that good deeds will grow in number just as fish do.

 Apples, honey and wine are all used in the celebrations

Next morning, synagogue services are very popular and attract large congregations. Many Jews who do not attend synagogue regularly will attend on this special day. The highlight of the service is the blowing of the shofar 100 times. This will be a mixture of short and long notes, culminating in a long final note of around ten seconds. The service itself is longer than normal and taken from a special holiday prayer book called the machzor.

A popular practice called Tashlikh takes place in the afternoon. It involves families going to a stream or river where there is flowing water and emptying their pockets out into the water. Small pieces of bread are often put in pockets especially for this. This symbolises casting off sins. It is thought to have its origins in the book of the prophet Micah:

Beliefs and teachings

... you will tread our sins underfoot and hurl all our iniquities into the depths of the sea.

Micah 7:19

If the first day of Rosh Hashanah occurs on Shabbat, this is done on the second day because carrying bread on Shabbat is forbidden and the flowing water may be further away than Jews are allowed to walk.

Research activity

Using the internet, try to find a recording of the shofar being blown.

AQA   Examiner's tip

If asked to write about the celebration of Rosh Hashanah, you can include both synagogue and home activities unless the question asks for one or the other.

Extension activity

Using information on these pages, list items and practices that are symbolic. Explain what each means.

Summary

You should now know and understand about the origins and celebration of Rosh Hashanah.

Activity

3   Imagine you are a young Jewish person. Write a letter to a friend telling them what you did the last time you celebrated Rosh Hashanah. Include how you felt and what you thought about at different points during the festival.

3.5 Yom Kippur (the Day of Atonement)

■ Celebration or commemoration?

Many people think of Yom Kippur as the most solemn day of the year because it involves reflecting on sins, fasting and asking God for forgiveness. Others see it as a more joyful event because through it they can have their sins forgiven and repair their relationship with God. There is no right or wrong response; it all depends on the person's own interpretation and perspective of the day. There is little doubt, though, that it is the holiest and most important day of the Jewish year.

■ Origins and purpose of Yom Kippur

Beliefs and teachings

You must deny yourselves and not do any work ... because on this day atonement will be made for you, to cleanse you. Then before the Lord you will be clean from all your sins. It is a sabbath of rest, and you must deny yourselves; it is a lasting ordinance.

Leviticus 16:29–31

The origins of Yom Kippur are in Leviticus 16, which sets out an elaborate ritual for observance of Yom Kippur. Part of it involves putting the sins of the people onto a goat and driving it into the desert, literally as a scapegoat. See Beliefs and teachings (right).

Following on from God writing down his judgement at Rosh Hashanah, Yom Kippur, the Day of Atonement, is the sealing of his book of judgement. Therefore, Yom Kippur is the last opportunity to appeal to God to change his judgement by demonstrating repentance before the book is sealed. The atonement that features in Yom Kippur is atonement between Jews and God. Atonement between each other must have been made in the days before Yom Kippur. Some people explain atonement as at-one-ment – becoming at one with God, or with others, through repentance.

Objectives

Know and understand the practices associated with Yom Kippur.

Beliefs and teachings

He (Aaron) shall bring forward the live goat. He is to lay both hands on the head of the live goat and confess over it all the wickedness and rebellion of the Israelites – all their sins – and put them on the goat's head. He shall send the goat away into the desert in the care of a man appointed for the task. The goat will carry on itself all their sins to a solitary place; and the man shall release it in the desert.

Leviticus 16:20–22

Research activity

Look at Leviticus 16:1–28 to find out more about this ritual.

⚭ links

For more about atonement and repentance see pages 58–59.

Activities

1. Explain the origins of Yom Kippur.
2. What is the meaning of atonement?

A *During the morning of the day before Yom Kippur, chickens are traditionally killed and given to the poor. Many give money to the poor instead*

Observance of Yom Kippur

No work is done on Yom Kippur. In addition, it is a time of total fasting, which lasts for 25 hours from before the day begins to after it has ended. Various other activities are prohibited including bathing (many Jews perform mikveh – a special spiritual cleansing by immersion a few hours before Yom Kippur begins), wearing leather shoes and having sexual intercourse. It is usual to wear white as a symbol of purity. The prophet Isaiah referred to sins becoming 'as white as snow' (Isaiah 1:18). Many Jewish men wear a kittel, a plain white garment kept to wear on Yom Kippur. This is the garment in which they will be buried.

B *The Yom Kippur machzor prayer book is bound in white leather*

Services in the synagogue

The first service for Yom Kippur is an evening service called Kol Nidre. This means 'all vows' and during the service, Jews ask God to cancel any vows they may make between themselves and God in the following year, which they cannot keep. This practice originates from the time of the Spanish Inquisition, especially between 1480 and 1530 when Jews living in Spain were forced to convert to Christianity and swear vows to follow the Christian faith or be killed. Many left the country and settled elsewhere. It is a sad part of the service and reminds Jews of the difficulties they have faced in being true to their religion.

Many Jews spend much of Yom Kippur in the synagogue. In an Orthodox synagogue, it is not unusual for services to begin at 8am and continue until mid afternoon. They resume in late afternoon, continuing until nightfall.

Throughout the day, the service is taken from the machzor (prayer book). One of the most important features is a general confession when all sins are confessed as a community using the word 'we' rather than 'I'. This is inserted into the Amidah prayer. In addition to specific sins, it includes a confession to cover every eventuality:

> 66 *Forgive us the breach of positive commands and negative commands, whether or not they involve an act, whether or not they are known to us.* 99

The final service is known as Ne'ilah (the closing of the gates). In ancient times, the gates of the Temple would have been closed at the end of prayer. The door of the ark is kept open throughout the Ne'ilah service, to symbolise the gates of the Temple, and so the congregation has to stand throughout the service. This is seen as the last chance to make confession before the ritual is over, atonement is complete and the book of judgement is finally sealed. The door of the Ark is then closed symbolising the closing of the gates of God's judgement. A long blast on the shofar signals the end of the fast.

Activities

3 Write a diary entry for Yom Kippur (10th Tishri) written by a 15-year-old Jewish person. Try to include how you felt during the fasting and the other observances of Yom Kippur.

4 Which do you think is the most important Yom Kippur observance? Give reasons why.

AQA **Examiner's tip**

Learning the detail and symbols of this ceremony will help you to remember the main meaning of Yom Kippur.

Discussion activity

With a partner spend a couple of minutes discussing whether you think Yom Kippur is a celebration or a commemoration. Try to come up with some reasons for your decision.

Extension activity

The book of Jonah from the Tenakh is often read during Yom Kippur. Read it for yourself (it is only short) and explain what it tells you about repentance.

Summary

You should now know and understand more about the origins, purpose and observance of Yom Kippur.

3.6 Pesach – origins and preparations

Origins of Pesach

Pesach is often referred to as Passover because it remembers the night when God passed over Egypt killing every first-born child and animal but not those of the Hebrews.

Pesach remembers an event that took place over 3,000 years ago when the Hebrews (or Jews) were slaves in Egypt. God chose Moses, a Hebrew who had been brought up in the household of the Pharaoh, to be their leader. God intended to rescue the Hebrews from slavery and helped them to leave slavery in Egypt to start a new life in Canaan – the Promised Land.

The story started with God appearing to Moses in the form of a burning bush that, even though in flames, was not damaged. God gave Moses instructions to go to the Pharaoh and ask him to allow the Hebrews to go into the desert for three days to make offerings to God.

Pharaoh refused and ordered them back to their work. He even made their work more difficult, which set the Hebrews against Moses, whereas before they had supported him. God then persuaded Moses to return to Pharaoh and threaten plagues upon Egypt until he allowed the Hebrews to leave. Pharaoh once again refused, so ten plagues followed. The first was the River Nile becoming red like blood, followed by plagues of frogs, gnats, flies, the death of livestock, boils, hail, locusts and darkness. The next plague was the most terrible and the one that finally persuaded Pharoah to let the Hebrews leave Egypt.

The Hebrews were instructed to make preparations to leave. This included selecting a lamb to sacrifice at twilight on the 14th day of the month, smearing some of its blood on their doorposts and roasting and eating the meat. They were also told that they should celebrate the coming event every year by eating unleavened bread (bread without yeast) for seven days. At midnight, that night, all the Egyptian first-born were killed as the Lord passed over the land. Pharoah changed his mind and the Hebrews were allowed to go free. Eventually, after miraculously crossing the Red Sea when God parted the water to allow them to walk across, and then many years of wandering in the wilderness of Sinai, they entered the land that God had promised them.

Preparations for Pesach celebration

Pesach is a joyful festival because it celebrates the birth of the nation of the Jews. God is seen as having fulfilled his promise to be their God by controlling history to bring them to the land he promised them. On the journey he gave them the Law, which made them his people. Pesach fulfils the instruction to have an annual celebration involving unleavened bread to mark the freedom this event brought them. It is also tinged with sadness, however, because it brings to mind a time of slavery and maybe also sadness over the death of the first-born Egyptians.

A *God spoke to Moses through a burning bush that was not damaged*

The most important preparation for Pesach is the removal of chametz (leaven) from the home. This is essential because during the seven days of the festival, nothing containing chametz can be eaten. Chametz is anything made from any of the five major grains including wheat, oats and barley, which has not been completely cooked within 18 minutes of coming into contact with water. This is because they swell while cooking, meaning they would not be unleavened as required by God. Also, it is symbolic of being 'puffed up with pride', which would be inappropriate during a festival marking a story that could not have happened without God. Some Orthodox Jews also avoid rice, corn, peanuts and beans during Pesach for the same reason.

Also on this day, some first-born male Jews fast to commemorate the fact that although first-born Hebrews were left unharmed, the Egyptian ones were killed.

B *Unleavened bread is a feature of Pesach*

Research activity

Read the story of the Jews leaving Egypt from Exodus 3:1–12:42 and reflect upon how God helped the Hebrews to escape.

Peter's story

'We have to remove all chametz from the house before Pesach starts. We all help Dad to collect all products containing chametz and utensils used to prepare chametz food; even pots, pans, crockery and cutlery. When they are all boxed up, Dad sells them to Alan, a non-Jewish workmate. Although Alan is not Jewish, he will look after them for us and allow Dad to buy everything back after Pesach has finished. I know this seems a little silly to a non-Jew but it is important because we cannot have chametz in the house and throwing everything away would be very wasteful. Anyway, why change what our ancestors have been doing for centuries? We then have to clean the house thoroughly to remove all possible traces of chametz. We all help with this task, which usually takes four or five days.

Straight after nightfall at the beginning of the day before Pesach (14th Nisan), my sisters and I hide ten pieces of bread around the house. We wrap them in paper so no crumbs can fall on our nicely cleaned floors. Dad has to look for them. He first says a blessing and then uses a candle, a feather to sweep up any crumbs, a wooden spoon to pick them up and a paper bag to put them in. We usually have to give him a few clues but eventually he finds all ten. Don't worry, this is just another of our customs. Next morning, Dad lights a fire in the garden and burns the bag containing the crumbs, candle, feather and wooden spoon. We now know that we have got rid of as much chametz as we possibly can.

C

Case study

Summary

You should now know and understand the origins of and preparations performed for Pesach.

Activities

3 What is chametz?

4 Explain why chametz is forbidden at Pesach.

A time of celebration

Pesach lasts a total of eight days. On the first and last two days, if possible, Jews will not go to work but during the middle four days they can work if it is considered important. However, chametz-free foods have to be eaten during the whole festival. The most important part of the festival occurs right at the beginning of the celebration on 15th Nisan with the Seder meal. This meal is not only a large celebration meal but it also has various specified symbolic elements that bring to mind the origins of the festival.

The Seder meal

The wife and mother of the house light candles to welcome the festival into the home. It is likely that some other members of the family visit the synagogue to offer thanks to God for his role in their escape from Egypt. When they arrive back home, the Seder meal begins with the recitation of the Kiddush blessing. On the table are red wine, three matzot (unleavened bread) and a special plate containing symbolic foods, which are eaten. There is also a copy of the Haggadah (a special book) which tells the story of Pesach, sets out the words that are said and the order in which the various items are eaten or drunk. The word Seder literally means 'order' because everything happens in the order laid out in the Haggadah. Some Jews may vary the order or items a little but most keep it as it is written.

The first glass (or goblet) of wine is blessed and drunk. The wine is red because it reminds Jews of the blood of the lambs that was smeared over the doorposts to keep their first-born safe and also the Hebrews' own blood that was shed in slavery. The family then wash their hands before they eat some vegetable (karpas) dipped in salt water. The salt water symbolises the tears Jews shed in slavery and the vegetable, often parsley, could remind the Jews of their lowly origins in Egypt or symbolise new life, which God gave them in the Promised Land. One of the three matzot is then broken in half. Part is returned to the pile while the other half is put aside for later and possibly hidden either by the children or the parents. The matzot is unleavened to obey God's command and also to remind Jews that prior to escaping from Egypt, the Hebrews did not have time to let their bread rise.

Beliefs and teachings

The Pesach Kiddush

Praised art thou, O Lord our God, King of the universe, who hast chosen us from all peoples and exalted and sanctified us with thy commandments. In love hast thou given us, O Lord our God, solemn days of joy and festive seasons of gladness, even this day of the Feast of Unleavened Bread, a memorial of the departure from Egypt. Thou hast chosen us for thy service and hast made us sharers in the blessings of thy holy festivals. Blessed art thou, O Lord.

www.sacred-texts.com

A *The Seder plate*

The story is then told, starting with the youngest person asking four questions about the proceedings. Each question start with 'Why is it different?' These questions are answered from the Haggadah throughout the rest of the meal as the story of the escape from Egypt is told. After this, the second glass of wine is blessed and shared. The hands are then washed again in preparation for eating the matzot, which is blessed before some is eaten. Bitter herbs (maror), usually horseradish, or a long lettuce is then eaten to represent the bitterness of slavery. It is dipped in charoset, which is a sweet mixture of apples, cinnamon, nuts and wine. It is made to look like the mortar used by the Hebrew slaves. Its sweet taste is a reminder that life now is sweet compared with slavery. Some Jews then eat a different bitter herb with charoset on a piece of matzah. It is at this point that the festive meal is usually eaten. There is no requirement about what this must contain, apart from the fact that there must be no chametz. Chicken or turkey are popular choices. Also on the Seder plate are two reminders of sacrifices the Jews used to offer in the temple – a burnt egg and a shank bone of a lamb or chicken.

Once the main meal has been eaten, the matzah (afikomen) that was earlier put aside or hidden has to be found by those who did not hide it and is shared with the others. Children are often given money or a small gift for finding it, if their parents have hidden it, or for offering clues to their parents if they have hidden it. This shows the emphasis on the role of the family and that, even on a serious occasion, Jews will introduce some humour especially to encourage their children to take part.

A third glass of wine is then poured and a prayer is said. The wine is then blessed and shared. A fourth and fifth glass are poured. The fifth one is poured for Elijah, who is expected to visit on Pesach to announce the coming of the Messiah, and is left undrunk. The door is opened for a while in case he appears. After reciting or singing some psalms, the fourth glass of wine is blessed and drunk before a simple statement is made, that the Seder has been completed, together with a wish that next year, those present may celebrate Pesach in Jerusalem.

After nightfall on the eighth and final day of Pesach, the Pesach utensils are packed away until next year and the ordinary ones and any chametz food is brought back. Somebody in the family usually bakes a cake to show that chametz foods can once more be eaten.

B   *A child's Haggadah showing slaves under Pharoah in Egypt*

Research activities

1   Try to find and watch some film of the Seder meal. You might look first at www.youtube.com

2   Find out why the last matzah is called 'afikomen'.

Extension activity

See what you can find out about a Haggadah book. How are the books made attractive for children.

Activities

1   Pick out all the actions and items from the Seder meal that are symbolic (represent something else). List them and what they each represent.

2   How do you feel about the use of wine in a Seder meal? Explain your opinion.

3   Why do you think Jews always express a wish that they should keep next year's Pesach in Jerusalem?

Summary

You should now know and understand the events and symbolism of the Seder meal.

AQA   Examiner's tip

If writing about the Seder meal, it is usually important to include the symbolic meaning of the food on the table.

3.8 Pilgrimage

Definition

A **pilgrimage** can be defined as a journey made for religious reasons. A person who makes such a journey is called a pilgrim. A place of pilgrimage is one which has some significance for the faith, maybe a place connected with a founder or some other important person. Perhaps a significant event happened there. Whatever the reason for the place becoming a place of pilgrimage, pilgrims are usually able to identify a special spiritual reason for visiting, often with long-lasting effects on their faith or outlook.

Discussion activities 👥👥👥

1 If you could visit any town or city on earth, where would it be? Share your idea with a partner and explain to them why you have chosen that specific one. Is it just because you think it is a nice place with good weather or are there other reasons why you might wish to visit – perhaps personal ones?

2 Now repeat this exercise but choose a building rather than a town or city.

Many religious pilgrimages are made to a specific building in a significant town or city. It is likely that the building may have been built especially to mark the reason why the place is important. Nowadays, it may have become rather commercialised with souvenir shops and cafes close by. Many pilgrims however will be greatly affected by their visit to a holy place and will be able to ignore the commercialism, reflecting on the spiritual importance of the place for their faith.

Activities

1 Why do you think places of pilgrimage have attracted sellers of 'rubbish souvenirs'?

2 Do you think people should be prevented from selling souvenirs and refreshments close to places of pilgrimage? Explain your answer.

3 'The spiritual importance of places of pilgrimage for believers cannot be damaged by commercialism.' What do you think? Explain your opinion.

The origins of Jewish pilgrimage

The Torah makes pilgrimage a duty for Jews. The book of Deuteronomy emphasises this:

Beliefs and teachings

Three times a year all your men must appear before the Lord your God at the place he will choose: at the Feast of Unleavened Bread (Pesach), the Feast of Weeks (Shavuot) and the Feast of Tabernacles (Sukkot). No man should appear before the Lord empty-handed: Each of you must bring a gift in proportion to the way the Lord your God has blessed you.

Deuteronomy 16:16–17

Dad, you told me this was an important religious site – why are there so many people selling rubbish souvenirs?

A

🔗 links

For more about pilgrimages to Jerusalem, see 3.9 and 3.10 pages 68–71.

Activities

4 Describe the decline of pilgrimage in Judaism from the time of the Torah to the present day.

5 What do you think has caused this decline?

6 Do you think pilgrimage, for some people, has become 'superstitious reverence for sacred spots'? Give your reasons.

These three pilgrimages became centred on Jerusalem and especially on the Temple. However, over time the duty to attend changed to a voluntary act that benefits the believer. In 70 CE, the Temple was destroyed by the Romans and many Jews left Israel to settle in Europe or other parts of the world. These acts of pilgrimage became much less important, especially as without the Temple, no sacrifices (gifts for God) could be offered. In 1948 after the Second World War, the state of Israel was established with its capital in Jerusalem. Today, most Jews still consider Jerusalem to be an important city for pilgrims.

B   *Pilgrims at Hebron*

Other pilgrimage sites

Almost all Jewish pilgrimage sites are in Israel or the Middle East. They tend to be tombs of prophets or other great Jewish figures and vary in importance in Jewish thinking. Some of them have synagogues close by (Jews never bury their dead within the walls of a synagogue), which have become a part of the pilgrim's visit. At Hebron, south of Jerusalem, are the tombs of Abraham and his family. Legend says that Abraham and his wife Sarah are buried in one tomb, their son Isaac and his wife Rebekah in another, with their son Jacob and his wife Leah in a third. The fourth tomb contains the remains of Adam and Eve. For this reason, Hebron has been referred to as a 'Holy City' and is the destination of both Muslim and Jewish pilgrims.

Throughout Israel are believed to be tombs of other prophets and rabbis responsible for the writing of the Talmud. There are also similar tombs in the countries now known as Iraq and Iran, which are not often visited at the moment for political reasons. In Egypt is the synagogue of Moses in Dammuh, south of the capital city Cairo. This site also contains an ancient Jewish scroll, which is respected and admired by the small number of Jewish pilgrims that visit.

Many modern Jews reject the idea of pilgrimage, saying that God cannot be found more in one place than another. They describe the practice of pilgrimage as 'superstitious reverence for sacred spots'.

Holocaust sites

Since the end of the Second World War, some concentration camps, especially the two at Auschwitz in Poland, have become places of pilgrimage. These have taken on a special meaning for Jews because many of them can trace their family back to discover relatives who were murdered in the gas chambers there. The government of Israel is keen that young Jews should visit these sites because they have become a tragic reminder of the fate of one-third of the world's Jewish population who were alive at the start of the Second World War. Shrines in memory of those who died have been established at the Auschwitz I and II camps.

Activity

7   'A pilgrimage is no more than a sightseeing holiday.' Do you agree? Give reasons for your answer, showing that you have thought about more than one point of view. Refer to Judaism in your answer.

AQA   *Examiner's tip*

Knowing about sites like Hebron will help you to understand why Jews make pilgrimages, and you can include it as an example in a general question. You will only be asked specific questions about two sites in Jerusalem – the Western Wall and Yad Vashem, which are described in 3.9 and 3.10 pages 68–71.

∞ **links**

For more about Auschwitz, including a photograph of the shrine at Auschwitz I see 6.10 pages 136–137.

Activity

8   Do you think that a place where more than a million people were murdered (Auschwitz) is an appropriate place for pilgrims to visit? Give your reasons.

Extension activity

'Pilgrimage should be a voluntary act that benefits believers.' Write down what you think about this statement from the point of view of a Jewish person.

Summary

You should now know and understand about pilgrimage and have evaluated the effects of pilgrimage and the need for it.

3.9 Jerusalem – The Western (Wailing) Wall

Jerusalem

As the historic place of pilgrimage in Judaism, Jerusalem is still considered an important city to visit. It is no longer a duty for a Jew to visit Jerusalem but many still choose to do this. In this way they believe they are maintaining the traditional practices of their faith. For many centuries, the Western Wall, the only remaining part of the Jewish Temple site, has been the focus of pilgrimage in Judaism and in the last 50 years the Yad Vashem Holocaust Memorial, established in 1953, has become another place of pilgrimage.

The Temple in Jerusalem

The first Temple was built by Solomon and completed in around 957 BCE. It contained the Holy of Holies (Kodesh Kodashim), which was believed by the Jews to be the holiest place on earth. Only the High Priest was allowed in there and then only once a year at the festival of Yom Kippur. The Holy of Holies in Solomon's Temple contained the Ark of the Ten Commandments. This was a wooden box overlaid with gold in which the Ten Commandments were kept. It was highly valued and respected by the Jews.

The Temple was destroyed by the Babylonians in 586 BCE. The Ark disappeared during Babylonian rule and so when the second Temple was completed in 515 BCE, the Holy of Holies remained empty. This Temple was attacked and seriously damaged in 54 BCE and rebuilt and enlarged soon after by Herod the Great. This Temple was destroyed in 70 CE by the Romans. There is now a mosque called 'The Dome of the Rock' on the site of the Temple.

The Western Wall

The Western Wall is a large piece of wall, more than 2,000 years old, which is the only remaining part of the perimeter wall of the Temple Mount enclosing the precinct of Herod's Temple. It is around 20 metres high and made of large blocks of stone, the largest being nearly 15 metres long and 5 metres high.

While the Temple was standing, it contained an altar, which was used by the Jews for the offering of sacrifices. At times such as Pesach, the altar was covered in blood from the thousands of lambs that were sacrificed there. Since the destruction of the Temple in 70 CE, no such sacrifices have been made because the altar was destroyed along with most of the rest of the Temple.

Jews believe that in making a pilgrimage to the Western Wall they are making a personal sacrifice in terms of time and money. However,

A *The Western Wall*

Objectives

Understand and evaluate the importance of the Western Wall as a place of pilgrimage.

links

See pages 104–105 for more information about Yad Vashem.

Activities

1 Briefly outline the story of the Temple, starting with Solomon and finishing with its role in the Messianic Age.

2 Why do you think Jews believe the Temple is so important?

there are other beliefs about the Temple of which Jews may be reminded on a visit to the Western Wall. Many Jews believe that at the end of history, the Messianic Age will be announced by the sounding of the ram's horn from the Temple Mount and the Jews will return to Jerusalem and rebuild the Temple.

Many Jewish people visit the Western Wall at special times in their lives, most particularly for their Bar Mitzvah. They feel it is appropriate for the boy to become a man at the most sacred site in Judaism and families will try to arrange a visit at the appropriate time if they can afford to.

∞ links

For more about Bar Mitzvah, see pages 104–105.

AQA   *Examiner's tip*

Remember that the Western Wall is from the wall around the Temple Mount and not from the Temple building itself.

Case study

Reuben

Reuben is a young Orthodox Jew living in North London. He is now 15 years old but remembers his Bar Mitzvah at the Western Wall as though it was yesterday.

'My father, grandfather and I arrived in Jerusalem on Monday afternoon. Unfortunately my mother and two sisters had to stay behind in London. As we are Orthodox Jews, they would not have been allowed to take part anyway. I was sorry about this but at least we had a special meal to celebrate my Bar Mitzvah when we got home. Although my 13th birthday was on a Tuesday, I had to wait until Thursday morning for my Bar Mitzvah. It didn't matter too much because there are plenty of other places to visit in Jerusalem. We saw the Dead Sea Scrolls in the museum and we also visited King David's tower. The Rabbi who took charge of my ceremony was very nice. He spoke to us in English when he explained what was going to happen, but, of course, as we are Orthodox Jews, the ceremony was in Hebrew. I think I understood most of it and I am sure I read from the Torah properly – I had practised enough! There were quite a lot of Orthodox Jews who stopped what they were doing and listened to me. It made me more nervous but it was nice of them to support me in that way. I cannot think of a better place for me to have become a man.

'My father thought it would be a good idea to spend my first full day as a "real" Jew at the Yad Vashem Holocaust memorial. I wasn't really looking forward to it but I am glad I went there because I think we need to show our respect to all those who died.'

Discussion activity 🏃🏃🏃

With a partner, spend three minutes discussing whether you feel that travelling to Jerusalem for Bar Mitzvah is a good use of time and resources. Focus on the benefits the boy may get from this visit.

   An Hasidic Jew praying at the Western Wall. Note the slips of paper (kvitlach) in the wall

Jews who make a pilgrimage to the Western Wall get as close to the wall as they can before offering their prayers. Many of them write messages or prayers on small slips of paper (kvitlach) and place them in cracks in the wall in the hope or expectation that they will be answered. Traditionally, the main part of the wall has been reserved for Orthodox Jewish men with smaller, less prominent parts reserved for Reform Jews and also for Orthodox women.

Research activity 🔍

Look at www.aish.com/wallcam for live pictures from the Western Wall. The website also has information about the Western Wall.

Activities

3   Think of ten words that might express the thoughts of an Orthodox Jew praying at the Western Wall.

4   How many of your words express joyful feelings and how many express sad feelings? Why do you think this is?

5   Write your own kvitlach message or prayer that you might leave at the Western Wall.

Summary

You should now understand and be able to evaluate the importance to Jewish people of the Western Wall in Jerusalem.

Origins of Yad Vashem

Yad Vashem is a Holocaust memorial, an archive of information including the names and testimonies of Holocaust victims and a museum dedicated to them. It was set up by the government of Israel in 1953 and is run by the Holocaust Martyrs' and Heroes' Remembrance Authority. It is situated on Har Hazikaron – the Mount of Remembrance in Jerusalem. The name is based on a verse in Isaiah 56:5:

> 66 *to them I will give within my temple and its walls*
> *a **memorial** and a **name***
> *better than sons and daughters ... that will not be cut off* 99

In Hebrew, 'yad' means memorial or hand and 'shem' means name.

Objectives

Know and understand about Yad Vashem.

Understand and evaluate the importance of Yad Vashem as a place of pilgrimage.

Key terms

Yad Vashem: a memorial to the Holocaust victims in Jerusalem – means 'a memorial and a name'.

∞ links

Find out more about the Holocaust in 6.9 and 6.10.

Activities

1. Why do you think the Government of Israel set up Yad Vashem within eight years of the end of the Second World War?
2. Isaiah 56:5 is thought to have been written around the 6th century BCE. Do you think the prophet was foreseeing the creation of Yad Vashem or some other event? Explain your reasons.

What is at Yad Vashem?

Yad Vashem contains the largest collection of material and documentation connected with the Holocaust. This includes written accounts, photographs and recorded testimonies of survivors. Many Jews visiting Yad Vashem hope to find out a little more about members of their families who died in the Holocaust from this archive. In addition to these resources, there is also a library containing more than 100,000 books and other publications connected with the Holocaust that can be accessed by visitors on site.

The Hall of Names remembers the victims of the Holocaust by name and not just as a number. Names and brief biographical data submitted by family members and friends on more than three million victims are recorded in the 'Pages of Testimony' and have been computerised so people can search online for their names. The International School for Holocaust Studies provides Holocaust education for students and teachers either on site at Yad Vashem or in their own schools and colleges by providing resources and visiting speakers.

The new Holocaust History Museum covers over 4,200 square metres. It presents the story of the Holocaust from the Jewish perspective and emphasises the experiences of victims through their own stories and possessions. There is also a Museum of Holocaust Art, which contains art inspired by the Holocaust and done by Holocaust survivors, some of it between 1939 and 1945.

A   *A sculpture at Yad Vashem showing Jewish children being protected by Janusz Korczak – who ran an orphanage in Poland. When 200 children from the orphanage were arrested and taken to a death camp at Treblinka in 1942, Korczak chose to go with them so they wouldn't die alone*

Memorial sites

Yad Vashem also has several memorial sites dedicated to victims. The Hall of Remembrance contains a memorial flame and a crypt containing the ashes of some of the victims. Names of death camps and concentration camps are written on the floor. Memorial ceremonies are held in this building, most notably the annual remembrance called 'Holocaust Martyrs' and 'Heroes' Remembrance Day' on 27–28 Nisan (late April or early May). There is also a Children's Memorial hollowed out in an underground cavern where memorial candles are lit to pay tribute to around 1.5 million children who were murdered in the death camps because they were not old enough to work. There is also a 2.5-acre monument called The Valley of the Communities, which has the names of over 5,000 Jewish communities that were destroyed engraved into the walls.

Yad Vashem also pays tribute and gives thanks to non-Jews who risked their lives to save Jews during the Holocaust. Two thousand trees have been planted alongside the Avenue of the Righteous Among the Nations. Each tree has a plaque naming and giving the nationality of non-Jews whose work for the Jews is worthy of honour. The Garden of the Righteous Among the Nations contains 19,000 names of non-Jews engraved on walls.

One of several sculptures throughout Yad Vashem is an original railway cattle car used to transport Jews to a death camp, perched on the edge of an abyss facing the Jerusalem forest. This is called the Memorial to the Deportees.

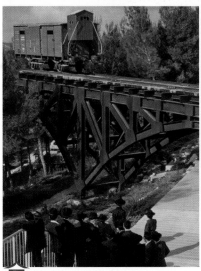

B *The Memorial to the Deportees*

Research activity

Find out more about Yad Vashem at www.yadvashem.org

Activities

3 Note down and describe some of the features of Yad Vashem.

4 Yad Vashem has a dual focus on education and remembrance. Which do you think is most important? Give reasons for your answers.

5 What do you think is the significance of the Memorial to the Deportees being perched on the edge of an abyss?

AQA Examiner's tip

Even if you decide that a visit to Yad Vashem is not really a pilgrimage, you may still use it as an example of pilgrimage in your examination.

Is Yad Vashem a place of pilgrimage?

Most Jews visit Yad Vashem to pay tribute not only to members of their family who perished during the Holocaust but also to fellow members of their faith. The idea of community is very strong in Judaism and it could be seen as a duty to pay tribute to the sacrifice of their spiritual brothers and sisters. Whether this can be called a pilgrimage is open to debate. However, for many Jews it is clearly a journey made for religious reasons so can properly be described as a pilgrimage, even if some do not see it as such. For other Jews, who perhaps do not have a strong religious faith, the visit may still be a pilgrimage in the sense that it is made to pay respect to those who died and remember them and the faith they held.

Discussion activity

With a partner, spend a few minutes discussing the importance of Yad Vashem for visitors, both Jews and non-Jews.

Extension activity

Do you think there is a need for a Holocaust memorial such as Yad Vashem? Give your reasons.

Summary

You should now know and understand about Yad Vashem and understand its importance as a place of pilgrimage.

3

Festivals and pilgrimage – summary

For the examination, you should now be able to:

✔ show knowledge and understanding of how festivals are celebrated in Judaism including:

 – Shabbat

 – Rosh Hashanah

 – Yom Kippur

 – Pesach

✔ consider the role of pilgrimage in Jewish tradition to include:

 – the Western Wall

 – Yad Vashem

✔ discuss festivals and pilgrimage from different points of view, including Jewish ones.

Sample answer

1 Write an answer to the following exam question.

'Pesach is the most important Jewish festival.' Do you agree? Give reasons for your answer, showing that you have thought about more than one point of view. *(6 marks)*

2 Read the following answer.

> Pesach is a very important festival but I don't think it is the most important. Certainly, it is important for Jews to celebrate the fact that God chose them to be his special people and gave them the Promised Land but all that was in the past. True Jews do still see themselves as God's people and should be grateful but I think Yom Kippur is more important. It is more difficult to live in a way that God wants us to nowadays, so the chance to repent and have our relationship with God restored is one that should be valued. If people don't care about being sinners, they shouldn't really be celebrating other festivals anyway.

3 With a partner, discuss the sample answer. Do you think that there are other things that the student could have included in the answer?

4 What mark would you give this answer out of six? Look at the mark scheme in the Introduction on page 7 (AO2). What are the reasons for the mark you have given?

AQA Examination-style questions

1   Look at the photograph below and answer the following questions.

(a)   Explain why Jews observe a weekly Shabbat.   *(3 marks)*

 You should write six to eight lines unless your writing is particularly small or large.

(b)   'A synagogue is the best place for Jews to celebrate a festival.'
What do you think? Explain your opinion.   *(3 marks)*

 In a three-mark evaluation question such as this, you only need to say what you think and explain why you think this. You do not need to give an alternative opinion.

(c)   Describe what happens at a Seder meal.   *(4 marks)*

 Because the word 'describe' is used, you do not need to explain what things mean.

(d)   'Celebrating festivals is more important than pilgrimage'. Do you agree? Give reasons for your answer, showing that you have thought about more than one point of view. Refer to Judaism in your answer.   *(6 marks)*

 To earn full marks you need to write a well-argued response with evidence of a reasoned consideration of two different points of view. You should show insight and apply your knowledge and understanding of Judaism effectively. You should also use examples of Jewish festivals and pilgrimages to support the point you are making.

4 Personal lifestyle

4.1 Lifestyle choices

A *A Jewish family celebration*

Objectives

Objectives

Explain what is meant by the term 'lifestyle' and what influences lifestyle choices.

Personal lifestyle

Personal lifestyle is the way in which someone chooses to live their life. Personal lifestyle might be described as what matters to that person: his or her attitudes. The lifestyle of an individual may include their choice of diet, dress, recreation, work, and home environment. There are all sorts of things that influence people's lifestyle choices: for some people one of the influences on the lifestyle that they choose might be their religion.

Discussion activities

1. List all the restrictions on your life that stop you from doing just what you want. These might include the law in the UK or school rules.

2. Share your list with the rest of the class. Discuss the class lists and why there are similarities and differences between them.

Research activity

Using the internet and/or library find out about the lifestyle of very Orthodox Jews.

Compile a factsheet that explains the lifestyle of Orthodox Jews.

links

For more information about the Torah, Talmud and Halakhah, see Chapter 1, pages 8–13.

B *Orthodox Jews in their traditional dress*

Jewish lifestyle choices

Jews make their lifestyle choices based on the Torah and Talmud because they believe that these contain God's laws, and to ignore these laws would be to disobey God. To ignore God's rules would be unacceptable and a sin. They are guided by the teachings of Judaism but there is diversity of opinion between Orthodox and Reform Jews as to what these lifestyle choices are, especially over diet, dress and Sabbath observance.

The lifestyle Jews choose depends on their interpretation of the Halakhah. The interpretation and application of the laws may vary from country to country and according to the branch of Judaism to which the Jew belongs. The culture of the country in which they live will have an influence on a Jew's lifestyle as well and sometimes there can be confusion between what is required by Judaism and what is the result of the influence of customs and traditions from the country in which they have been brought up. For this reason the family plays a very important part in educating children to understand the lifestyle choices a Jew should make.

∞ links

For more information about the importance of the family in Judaism, see Chapter 5, pages 96–99.

∞ links

For more information about kosher food in Judaism, read pages 76–77 of this chapter.

Activities

1. Explain what is meant by a personal lifestyle.
2. Explain what factors will influence a Jew's personal lifestyle choices.
3. 'It does not matter in which country you live; it is the way you live your life that matters.' Do you agree? Give reasons for your answer, showing that you have thought about more than one point of view. Include religious views in your answer.

Activity

4. Read the case study on Reform Jews in the UK. Explain in your own words how manufacturers in the UK are helping Jews keep the Kosher rules.

Reform Jews in the UK

Case study

To accommodate Jewish people, manufacturers produce ranges of products that are specially supervised. These cover such basics as bread through to frozen meals. Without recognised supervision, Orthodox Jews will not consume the product. If a product is marked as 'vegetarian', while it may be vegetarian, not having supervision means the food cannot be traced to its origins, e.g. it may be made on the same factory line as something that is not kosher, e.g. shellfish, and so Orthodox Jewish people would refrain from eating it. When it comes to eating out, special care and attention is placed on establishments that are specially supervised. Just like pre-made food, restaurants need to have supervision. Many Orthodox Jews will only eat out in a restaurant which is supervised by a Jewish authority; however less Orthodox Jews may feel comfortable eating in a restaurant, which is not supervised, provided they are not offered any product which conflicts with basic dietary laws.

(An explanation of the Kosher rules from the Jewish UK online magazine, Something Jewish*)*

C   *It is possible to find kosher food in UK supermarkets*

Summary

You should now be able to explain what is meant by personal lifestyle, and to understand some ways in which lifestyle choices are important.

AQA   *Examiner's tip*

Make sure that you are able to show an understanding of the Jewish views on an acceptable lifestyle.

4.2   Kosher and trefah

■ Kosher

Jews have to follow strict rules as to what they can and cannot eat. Food that is acceptable is called **kosher** food. The word 'kosher' means 'fit' or 'correct' and certain meat, such as pork, or combination of foods, such as eating dairy products at the same time as meat, are considered 'unfit' in Judaism.

The expression 'not Kosher' is sometimes used to refer to other things that are considered unacceptable according to Jewish law, such as certain forms of dress or actions, but the correct use of the term is to refer to food that is acceptable in Judaism. Some Jews use the word 'kashrut' rather than kosher to refer to acceptable food. Food that is not kosher is called **trefah**. The word means 'torn' and was originally used to describe animals that had been attacked and killed by a predator, that is the meat had been 'torn' from the animal carcass.

■ Why do Jews observe kosher laws?

The kosher laws are based on the laws found in the Torah and therefore Jews believe that they come from God. Some of the laws seem to be for hygiene or health reasons and others because an animal is more valuable for uses other than food. For example, the camel, which is trefah, is very important as a beast of burden that is able to cross deserts. So camels were valued for their uses for humans and not seen as sources of food. Therefore, Leviticus 11:3–4 states that the camel is ceremonially unclean (see page 78).

There have been various suggestions as to why the kosher and trefah laws benefit health. For example, by not eating animals that are unconscious before they are killed, it reduces the risk of eating an unhealthy animal. In the past, pigs carried many diseases and therefore, in a hot climate, the prohibition against eating pork was a wise one. However, health is not the only reason for keeping the dietary laws and many Jews would argue that the laws are kept simply because God has instructed which foods are kosher and which are not.

A *Camels are important as beasts of burden*

■ Kosher butchers

The animals and birds that Jews are permitted to eat only become kosher if they have been slaughtered in the prescribed manner. Each animal must be healthy and slaughtered by a rabbi called a shochet, who has been specially trained to ensure that animals are slaughtered in the correct manner to be kosher. The animal to be slaughtered must be healthy. A very sharp smooth-bladed knife (chalef) must be used to

Objectives

Know and understand what is meant by kosher and trefah food in Judaism.

Evaluate the kosher method of slaughtering animals.

Key terms

Kosher: food that meets Jewish laws.

Trefah: forbidden food – means 'torn'.

🔗 **links**

For more information about the sources of law in Judaism see Chapter 1, pages 8–26.

🔗 **links**

For more information about the dietary laws in Judaism see pages 78–79 of this chapter.

slit the animal's throat in such a way that the animal does not suffer. The blood must be removed from the animal as the Torah instructs that Jews must not eat blood. Even if the animal has been slaughtered correctly, certain parts of the animal must be removed as there are parts of the animal that are trefah and must not be eaten. These parts include fats found on the flanks of animals and certain internal organs such as the kidneys and intestines.

Excerpt taken from RSPCA Religious Slaughter Information Sheet (February 2009)

The RSPCA recognises that religious beliefs and practices should be respected. We also believe that it is important to ensure that animals are slaughtered under the most humane conditions possible. Scientific research has clearly demonstrated that slaughter of an animal without stunning can cause unnecessary suffering. Accordingly, the RSPCA is opposed to the slaughter of any food animal without first rendering it insensible to pain and distress until death supervenes.

We continue to press for changes in legislation that would improve the welfare of the animals at the time of slaughter. Until this occurs, the RSPCA proposes that:

- The Jewish and Muslim communities in the UK should review their slaughter practices. In New Zealand, for example, all animals slaughtered by the Halal method are stunned before slaughter and all animals slaughtered by the Kosher method are stunned shortly after the incision is made in the animal's neck. The progress already made in the UK in these areas should be extended to cover all animals slaughtered.

- All meat produced from animals that have not been stunned before slaughter should be clearly labelled in some way, so that it can be identified by consumers. The RSPCA believes that consumers have the right to choose whether or not they wish to buy meat from animals slaughtered without pre-stunning.

(Full RSPCA information sheet available online at www.rspca.org.uk)

B   *The Kosher symbol appears on food packaging*

C   *Animals that have 'split hooves and chew their cud' are kosher*

Activities

1. Explain what is meant by kosher food in Judaism.
2. 'Rules about what you eat help to strengthen faith.' What do you think? Explain your opinion.
3. Write an answer to the following question: 'Jews living in the UK should accept the pre-stunning of animals about to be slaughtered.' Do you agree? Give reasons for your opinion, showing that you have thought about more than one point of view. Remember to consider the Jewish beliefs about kosher meat in your answer.

AQA Examiner's tip

Make sure that you are able to explain what is meant by the terms 'kosher' and 'trefah'. These are key terms and you may be asked to explain them.

Summary

You should now be able to define what is meant by kosher and trefah food in Judaism, and to reflect on issues related to the practice.

4.3 Dietary laws

You may eat any animal that has a split hoof completely divided and that chews the cud. There are some that only chew the cud or only have a split hoof, but you must not eat them. The camel, though it chews the cud, does not have a split hoof; it is ceremonially unclean for you.

Leviticus 11: 3–4

Activities

1. Read the extract from Leviticus 11:3–4.
2. Write a summary of these rules.
3. Based on this passage, list three animals that can be eaten by Jews and three animals that God has forbidden as food.

The dietary laws

The Jewish dietary laws are called kashrut and the food that meets these laws is kosher. The kashrut is based on the laws found in the Torah, particularly the books of Deuteronomy and Leviticus. The Torah passages state what may and may not be eaten by Jews. The Talmud develops in more detail how Jews are to put these laws into practice. Orthodox Jews continue to believe these rules to be important to keep in modern society but many Reform Jews believe that they are now outdated and it is up to an individual as to whether or not they follow all the rules. Most Jews, however, continue to refrain from eating pork.

Kosher food

If the meat has been killed in the correct manner then kosher food includes:

- cows, sheep, goats and deer
- chicken, turkey, geese and quail
- fish that has scales and fins, such as salmon, tuna, carp, herring and cod.

Kosher food also includes:

- soft cheese and certain hard cheeses
- any fruit and vegetables, so long as they are free of insects.

Objectives

Know and understand the Jewish dietary laws.

links

Remind yourself of the meaning of kosher by re-reading pages 76–77 of this chapter.

Beliefs and teachings

Then God said, I give you every seed-bearing plant

on the face of the whole earth and every tree that

has fruit with seed in it. They will be yours for food.

Genesis 1:29

links

There are more details about the Torah and Talmud in Chapter 1, pages 8–11.

Discussion activity

As a whole class, discuss whether or not the Jewish dietary laws are outdated in the 21st century. Remember to include religious reasons to support your opinions.

A *Fish with fins and scales are kosher*

Trefah food

Food that is trefah (not kosher) and forbidden under Jewish law includes:

- pork, camel, rabbit, rodents and reptiles
- any animal that died of natural causes
- eagles, hawks and vultures
- seafood without fins and scales such as crabs, prawns, lobsters, oysters and clams
- any insects
- amphibians such as frogs
- most hard cheeses.

B   *Crabs do not have fins and scales so they are trefah*

Alcohol

Jews are not forbidden from drinking alcohol and they may drink any alcohol so long as it is kosher, i.e. made according to the dietary laws. Orthodox Jews drink wine only from grapes grown on vines that are over four years old, with nothing else growing near to them. Only Jewish men must harvest and process the grapes and any additives or utensils must be kosher. After it is bottled, it must still be handled only by Jews if it is to remain as kosher wine, unless the wine was boiled before it was bottled. Reform Jews are less strict about the handling of Jewish wine once it has left the vineyard.

Research activity

Using the internet and/or library, find out more about the different beliefs surrounding the use of alcohol in Judaism. Create a factsheet that explains the different opinions within Judaism about the use of alcohol. Remember to include Orthodox and Reform opinions in your factsheet.

Activity

4   Divide a piece of paper into two columns, one headed kosher and the other trefah. From the information in this section about Jewish dietary laws, list the foods in the correct columns according to whether they are considered to be kosher or trefah.

C   *Jews may drink wine so long as it is kosher*

AQA Examiner's tip

The key to good answers is often good examples. Find examples of foods that will be kosher and foods that will be trefah.

Summary

You should now be able to explain the dietary laws in Judaism.

4.4 The Jewish kitchen

◼ Combining foods

There are not only foods that Jews must never eat; there are also foods that must never be eaten together. This mainly applies to meat and milk products. After eating kosher meat, there must be a gap of several hours before anything containing milk is eaten. If food containing milk is eaten then there must be short gap before anything containing meat is eaten. This means that even if the beef was kosher, a Jew could not eat a beefburger and milkshake at the same time. The reasons for the law against combining meat and milk are debated in Judaism but most Jews believe that it is related to the instruction in Exodus 23:19 not to eat a goat in its mother's milk.

Discussion activity 👤👤👤

1 Look at Photo A of a beefburger and milkshake. As a whole class discuss why many Jews would consider this combination of food to be trefah, besides the fact that they are mixing meat and milk at the same time.

Discussion activity 👤👤👤

2 Discuss what you think may be the problems in eating kosher food for a Jewish teenager living in the UK.

During the week of Passover, Jews must not eat anything containing yeast, as an act of devotion to God. Many Jews not only avoid food containing yeast but also many foods that contain barley, rye, wheat and oats. Some Jews also avoid the use of rice during Passover. Not only must they not eat these items but they also must not allow them to come into contact with any of the food that they are going to eat during the period. This means that before Passover begins the house is cleared of all the foodstuffs that the family is not going to eat during Passover.

∞ links

To find out more about why yeast is forbidden during Passover read Chapter 3, pages 62–63.

◼ Utensils

During Passover the houses and particularly the kitchen are thoroughly cleaned to ensure that there is no possibility of food that is to be eaten made 'unfit' by coming into contact with food that is not to be eaten during Passover. Many Jewish households have a separate set of cutlery, crockery and kitchen utensils that they only use during the Passover week.

The fact that dairy and meat products must not be combined means that utensils used for meat preparation need to be kept separate from those utensils that come into contact with milk. This means that most Jewish households have two sets of utensils: one for use with meat dishes and one for dairy products. Jews need to ensure that other items in the kitchen such as tea towels, dishcloths, chopping boards and dish drainers remain kosher. Some Jews colour-code their kitchen utensils red and blue so that they know which items

A *Why would this combination of foods be trefah for Orthodox Jews?*

may be used to prepare or serve meat dishes and which are for use with dairy products. Jews may have a double sink in their kitchens so that they can wash the milk and meat utensils separately.

Utensils can be made kosher by heating them at a very high temperature or soaking them in water for several days.

A problem for many Jews living in non-Jewish communities is to make sure that when they eat out not only is the food kosher but also the utensils used to prepare the food as well as the dishes on which the food is served. Most synagogues will have kosher kitchens in which food can be prepared according to the Jewish dietary laws for functions held at the synagogue.

B *Dishes used for meat have to be kept and cleaned separately from those used for dairy products*

C *Why might eating in a restaurant be a problem for some Jews?*

Activities

1 Explain how a Jewish kitchen is organised to follow the Jewish dietary laws.

2 Explain how the celebration of Passover will affect the organisation of a Jewish kitchen.

3 Explain the problems that might arise in keeping the Jewish dietary laws for Jews living in non-Jewish countries.

Extension activity

Using the internet and/or library, find out what might be the health reasons for some of the dietary laws.

Research activity

Using the internet and/or library, find out more about how Jews keep a kosher kitchen.

Imagine that you are a Jewish journalist and write an article entitled 'How to keep a kosher kitchen' for a Jewish magazine.

Summary

You should now be able to explain how the dietary laws affect the preparation of food in Judaism.

4.5 Shabbat observance

■ A day of rest

The Fourth Commandment instructs Jews that they are not to work during Shabbat hours. Shabbat begins at sunset on Friday evening and ends at sunset on Saturday evening. This can be a problem for Jews living in the West, as dusk comes early in winter and their employers may expect them to continue to work after the Shabbat has begun. Some Jewish communities have standardised the Shabbat hours as 6pm Friday to 6pm Saturday to overcome this problem.

■ What actions are classed as work?

Jews do not agree, however, as to what is to be classed as work during the Shabbat. For example, some Orthodox Jews unplug the telephone in their homes during Shabbat as they consider that answering it would be classed as working on the Shabbat. Other Jews cook all the food before the Shabbat begins such as the special challah bread eaten on the Sabbath. This is because they consider cooking to be a form of work since they will have to light the cooker and lighting a fire is forbidden.

There are 39 categories of actions classified as work and therefore forbidden on the Shabbat. These categories are based on the Mishnah, which has formed the basis of the Halakhah. The one thing that these forbidden activities have in common is that they are all in some way creative actions or activities that control the environment in which the Jew lives. The actions are divided into four main groups of actions. These are activities required to bake bread; activities required to make clothes; activities required to make leather; and activities required to build a house. A decision has to be made about any activity that is not listed in the 39 categories as to whether or not it is classified as work and can or cannot be performed during Shabbat. One example is the activity of watching television.

Research activity 🔍

Using the internet and/or library find out the 39 categories of activities forbidden on the Shabbat.

Divide the 39 categories according to the four main groups of actions to which they belong.

Activity

1. Using the information you found out from the research activity, write an explanation of why you think that the following activities are not performed by some Jews on the Shabbat because they class them as work: turning on an electric light, watching television, opening a packet of crisps, sewing on a button and gardening.

Objectives

Know and understand how Jews observe Shabbat as a day of rest.

Evaluate the different views in Judaism about observing Shabbat as a day of rest.

⬭⬭ links

For more details of worship during the Sabbath (Shabbat) read Chapter 2, pages 44–45 and Chapter 3, pages 54–55.

⬭⬭ links

Remind yourself of the Fourth Commandment by rereading it (see page 54).

A *Can Jews watch television during Shabbat?*

B *Challah: the traditional bread eaten by Jews during Shabbat*

⬭⬭ links

For more details of the Mishnah and Halakhah read Chapter 1, pages 10–13.

Shabbat in the 21st century

Jews living in the 21st century have to decide what activities today are forbidden on the Shabbat by applying the 39 categories to life in the modern world. The result is that Jews have come to different conclusions as to what are acceptable activities on the Shabbat. For example many Jews consider that driving during Shabbat hours is wrong because it involves moving a vehicle and igniting the fuel, both of which are actions forbidden as work on the Shabbat. However, this causes a problem for Jews who do not live within walking distance of the synagogue. Many Reform Jews will use their cars to attend the synagogue if they live too far away to walk, whereas many Orthodox Jews will ensure that they live within walking distance of a synagogue. However, they would be allowed to use a vehicle if it was an emergency and could save someone's life.

Although there are restrictions on what Jews can do on the Shabbat, it is intended as a day of enjoyment and so Jews are encouraged to play games, spend time with their families and to go for walks. Some Jews have a short sleep in the afternoon to ensure that they have rested. It is also a day of worship and so Jews are encouraged to read the Torah as well as attending the Shabbat services in the synagogue.

Taking exercise during Shabbat

'While there are certain restrictions on Shabbat activity, there is a special mitzvah called "Oneg Shabbat" – which means a person should do what is enjoyable on Shabbat! Actually, if a person is exercising for enjoyment, it is permitted to exercise on Shabbat. One should be careful, however, not to push himself too much, because to get sweaty and overexerted goes against the spirit of rest and serenity that Shabbat is designed to provide.'

(Orthodox Rabbi Shraga Simmons)

Case study

C Exercise such as taking a walk for enjoyment is permitted during Shabbat

Activities

2 Explain how Jews observe Shabbat.

3 'Having a compulsory day of rest each week is a good idea.' What do you think? Explain your opinion.

4 'Answering a mobile phone is not work.' Explain why an Orthodox Jew may not agree with this statement.

Extension activity

'The rules of Shabbat are outdated in the 21st century.' Do you agree? Give reasons for your opinion showing that you have thought about more than one point of view, including the opinions of Orthodox and Reform Jews.

Summary

You should now be able to explain how Jews observe the Shabbat as a day of rest and to evaluate the different views within Judaism about this observance.

AQA Examiner's tip

Make sure that you are able to explain the importance of Shabbat observance in Judaism.

4.6 The kippah

What is a kippah?

The **kippah** is also known as a capel or a yarmulkah. Yarmulkah translates as 'in awe of the Lord' and therefore is a reminder that God is always above the wearer. In Hebrew kippah means 'dome'. The plural of kippah is kippot.

The kippah is a small, slightly rounded brimless skull cap that is worn by Jewish men and, in the Reform tradition, some women. It may be small and only cover the back of the head whereas other kippot may be much larger and cover the whole crown of the head. Orthodox Jews will wear it continually whereas other Jews may only wear it during prayers, Torah study and eating.

Objectives

Know and understand the importance of the kippah in Judaism.

Key terms

Kippah: a skull cap.

A A Jewish man wearing a kippah

Beliefs and teachings

Cover your head in order that the fear of heaven may be upon you.

Talmud: Shabbat 156b

Why do Jews wear a kippah?

Jews believe that when they wear the kippah they are obeying the instruction in the Talmud: Shabbat 156b. By wearing the kippah Jews are showing their submission to God and are reminded that God is always above them. It also shows acceptance of the 613 laws from God and acts as an outward sign that the person is a Jew.

The colour and design of the kippah may show the branch of Judaism or community to which the Jew belongs. Some Jews, especially groups of Orthodox Jews, will wear a hat over the kippah.

B *The design of the kippah may show the community to which the Jew belongs*

A Jewish teenager talks about the importance of the kippah

'My name is Aaron and I have worn my kippah as long as I can remember. I live in Manchester and I am a follower of Manchester United football team, so I like to wear my kippah that has red and white stripes. Even though these are the colours of the football team I support, by wearing my kippah I never forget that the most important thing in my life is to worship God at all times and that God is above me. I am proud that by wearing my kippah I am showing people that I am proud to be a Jew. Although I was born in England I never forget that I am linked to a religion that has lasted for centuries and began in Israel. There is no problem with me wearing my kippah for school, as the school realises that it is an important part of my religion to wear this head-covering. I am glad I do not live in France where I would be banned from wearing it to school because they do not allow students to wear any religious dress.'

C

D *Jewish boys are encouraged to wear a kippah from an early age*

Activities

1 Describe a kippah.

2 Explain why Jews wear a kippah.

3 'Kippahs should not be allowed in schools.' What do you think of this statement? Explain your opinion.

4 'A kippah is an excellent way of showing the importance of one's faith.' Do you agree? Give reasons for your answer showing that you have thought about more than one point of view.

Extension activity

Using the internet and/or library find out why some Jews wear two head coverings: a kippah and a hat.

AQA Examiner's tip

Make sure that you can discuss the reasons why Jews are happy to wear a kippah.

Summary

You should now be able to explain the importance of the kippah in Judaism.

4.7 Orthodox dress

Beliefs and teachings

Do not wear clothes of wool and linen woven together.

Deuteronomy 22:12

Modesty in Judaism

Whatever Jewish men and women wear must be modest: although what is considered to be modest varies between Jewish communities. Some rabbis have drafted laws of modesty for their community or country. In Israel, for example, the Orthodox rabbis have stated the acceptable thickness of women's stockings and the acceptable length of women's earrings. Another Orthodox rule states that a woman's skirt must fall at least 10 centimetres (4 inches) below the knee, must not have side vents or be wrap-around.

Orthodox Jewish men are also expected to be modest in their dress and therefore they will usually wear long trousers and long-sleeved shirts. Some very Orthodox Jews called Haredi Jews will not wear shorts or T-shirts and tend to wear dark suits and white shirts. In addition Haredi and some strict Orthodox Jews called Hasidic Jews have beards and wear long side locks (peyote) as an outward sign of their Jewish faith. They believe that God instructed in Leviticus 19:27 that men must not cut off the hair at the side of the head or trim their beards.

Beliefs and teachings

Do not cut the hair at the sides of your head or clip off the edges of your beard.

Leviticus 19:27

Some Jews, particularly the Haredi Jews, believe that married women should cover their hair in public. Some Haredi Jewish women will even shave their heads after marriage, and cover their heads with a scarf or wig. It is usual for all Orthodox women to cover their heads when they attend synagogue services.

Research activity 🔍

Using the internet research the Orthodox Jewish rules of modesty for women.

Write an explanation of why you think these rules have been devised by the rabbis.

Beliefs and teachings

A woman must not wear men's clothing, nor a man wear women's clothing, for the Lord your God detests anyone who does this.

Deuteronomy 22:5

Objectives

Know and understand why there is Orthodox dress in Judaism.

🔗 links

Remind yourself of the dietary restriction about combining food in Judaism by re reading pages 80–81 in this chapter.

A *A Hasidic Jew*

Activity

1 Read the quotation from Deuteronomy 22:5. Explain the rule about male and female clothing based on this passage.

Mixing wool and linen

It is not only certain foods that Jews are not allowed to mix, but also it is forbidden in Judaism to mix wool and linen. This prohibition is called shatnez. Jews are not sure why this combination is forbidden but apply it not only to clothes but also to blankets and rugs. Therefore Jews must wear clothes that are either 100 per cent wool or 100 per cent linen. Wool refers only to wool from sheep and linen from the flax plant. This rule applies to any clothes that Jews might wear, including any clothes hired such as suits to wear at a wedding. A combination of other materials is permitted. Although wool and linen must not be mixed within one garment, it is acceptable for Jews to wear both materials. For example a woman could wear a wool jumper and linen blouse.

B *Jews may not combine lamb's wool with linen*

Kittel

A kittel is a white knee-length over garment that is worn by Orthodox prayer leaders and some Jews on holy days, such as the Passover Seder, and some grooms wear one under the wedding canopy. Some Jewish males are buried in a kittel as part of their burial garments. The white colour is said to symbolise purity and humility. Women often wear white on these days as well.

A Jewish teenager talks about wearing modest dress

Case study

'My name is Ruth. I am 16 and I live in London. I am very interested in fashion and many people think that because I am a Reform Jew, I will not be able to wear modern clothes. I can wear what I like so long as the skirt is not too short or the top is not too revealing. There are lots of online shops that sell fashionably modest clothing so I have no problem in buying clothes that I can wear when I go out with my friends. We are not allowed to mix wool and linen together in the same item of clothing but we can wear wool and linen at the same time. I have a linen jacket that I love to wear with a wool skirt. I do not feel that I have any problem in wearing modest dress and following the latest fashions.'

Discussion activity 👥

Organise a class debate to discuss the statement 'It does not matter matter what you wear so long as you worship God.' You must include reference to the views of Jews in your discussion.

∞links

Find out more about Jewish burial practice by reading Chapter 5, page 114–115.

Activities

2   Explain the Jewish rule about the use of wool and linen for clothing.

3   Why do some Jews wear a kittel?

4   'It would be very difficult for an Orthodox Jewish teenage girl living in Britain to keep to the rules of modest dress.' Do you agree? Give reasons for your answer, showing that you have thought about more than one point of view.

AQA Examiner's tip

When you are asked a straightforward question always answer the question directly. The answer to 'Why should Jewish women wear modest dress?' should begin with: 'Jewish women should wear modest dress because…' This helps to make sure you keep to the point.

Summary

You should now be able to explain Jewish views of orthodox dress and evaluate these views.

4.8 The mezuzah

Beliefs and teachings

Hear, O Israel: The Lord our God, the Lord is one.
Love the Lord your God with all your heart and with
all your soul and with all your strength. These
commandments that I give you today are to be upon
your hearts. Impress them on your children. Talk about
them when you sit at home and when you walk along the
road, when you lie down and when you get up. Tie them
as symbols on your hands and bind them on your foreheads.
Write them on the doorframes of your houses and on your gates.

Deuteronomy 6:4–9

What is a mezuzah?

A **mezuzah** is the scroll containing a handwritten parchment that is
found in a small box attached to the door post(s) of Jewish homes.
The word 'mezuzah' takes its name from the Hebrew for 'doorpost'.
Jews believe that by having this box they are obeying God's command
in Deuteronomy 6.9. Some Jews only put a mezuzah on the right door
post of the front door, whereas other Jews will put a mezuzah on every
door frame in the house.

Inside the mezuzah case is a handwritten kosher parchment
containing Hebrew verses from the Torah. The verses have to be from
Deuteronomy 6:4–9 and 11:13–21. The Shema is taken to be verses
6:4–9. On the back of the scroll one of the biblical names for God is
written. The name must be written with the respect that is to be shown
when writing God's name in Judaism. The scroll is rolled so that the
first letter of the name of God is visible.

When a mezuzah is fixed to the door frame, there is a small ceremony
called the Dedication of the House and a brief blessing is given.

Objectives

Identify and explain the
significance of the mezuzah in
Judaism.

⊙⊙ links

For more information about the
Torah, see Chapter 1, pages 8–9.

Key terms

Mezuzah: a scroll, containing the
Shema.

A *A mezuzah on a door post*

⊙⊙ links

For more information about the
Shema, see Chapter, 1, pages 14–15.

B *A mezuzah contains extracts from the Torah*

Beliefs and teachings

So if you faithfully obey the commands I am giving you today to love the Lord your God and to serve Him with all your heart and with all your soul – then I will send rain on your land in its season, both autumn and spring rains, so that you may gather in your grain, new wine and oil. I will provide grass in the fields for your cattle, and you will eat and be satisfied.

Be careful, or you will be enticed to turn away and worship other gods and bow down to them. Then the Lord's anger will burn against you, and He will shut the heavens so that it will not rain and the ground will yield no produce, and you will soon perish from the good land the Lord is giving you. Fix these words of mine in your hearts and minds; tie them as symbols on your hands and bind them on your foreheads. Teach them to your children, talking about them when you sit at home and when you walk along the road, when you lie down and when you get up. Write them on the doorframes of your houses and on your gates, so that your days and the days of your children may be many in the land that the Lord swore to give your forefathers, as many as the days that the heavens are above the earth.

Deuteronomy 11:13–21

Extension activity

Read Deuteronomy 6:4–9 and 11:13–21. Explain why you think that these passages are the ones chosen for the mezuzah.

AQA **Examiner's tip**

Remember that it is the scrolls within the mezuzah box that are the actual mezuzah.

■ How is the mezuzah used?

Having a mezuzah beside the front door is a visible sign that the house is the home of a Jewish family. As a Jew passes a mezuzah he or she will touch it and then kiss their fingers. By performing this action a Jew is showing love, respect and obedience to God. The mezuzah is a constant reminder of the need to obey God's commandments. When Jews move house they usually take their mezuzah(s) with them, so that there is no risk of the new owners showing disrespect to God's words. The fact that most Jews have a mezuzah on their door posts is a reminder to them of the unity of the Jews as God's people.

C *The Door of a Synagogue in Rhodes, Greece*

Activities

1 What is a mezuzah?
2 Why are mezuzahs placed on Jewish door posts?
3 How are mezuzahs used by Jews?

Summary

You should now be able to describe and explain the significance of a mezuzah.

4.9 The work of the Bet Din

■ The Bet Din

Within a Jewish community, the **Bet Din** (the Jewish religious court) will deal with matters of a specific Jewish nature. There are separate Bet Din for each of the main branches of Judaism in the UK, such as the Orthodox and Reform traditions. As far as the personal lifestyle of a Jew is concerned the Bet Din deal with matters that include:

- making valid the religious bills of divorce
- supervising conversions to Judaism
- resolving civil disputes
- resolving religious disputes
- providing kosher certification
- making judgments on current issues related to medical ethics.

Divorce

The document required for a **divorce** in Jewish law is called a get. It is handwritten in Hebrew and signed by two witnesses. The get is handed by the husband to the wife in front of witnesses. For the divorce to be recognised in the Jewish community, both partners must agree to it. Such a divorce would not be legal under UK law and therefore the couple would still have to have a civil divorce. Once the couple have received a get, they are free to remarry under Jewish law. The Bet Din will help the couple to make decisions about how their property is to be divided, and provision for any children.

Conversion to Judaism

Jewish converts are not only accepting the Jewish faith but also are becoming members of the Jewish community. After studying with a rabbi all aspects of the Jewish faith and lifestyle the convert will appear before the Bet Din, who will confirm that the three requirements for conversion to Judaism are met.

Objectives

Know, understand and be able to explain how the work of the Bet Din influences the personal lifestyle of a Jew.

⊙⊙ **links**

For more information about the Bet Din see Chapter 1, page 13.

Key terms

Bet Din: religious court, made up of rabbis.

Divorce: legal ending of a marriage.

A Jewish couples in the UK require a civil divorce as well as a get

Case study

The Bet Din in the USA

The Bet Din of America arranges Jewish divorces through the get (writ of divorce) process. The Bet Din ensures that the get procedure is carried out in a sensitive and caring manner, respects the dignity of all participants in the process and adheres to the highest standards of Jewish law to ensure the universal acceptance of gittin [what is good] administered under its auspices. The Bet Din also takes an active role in resolving cases involving spouses who refuse or are reluctant to deliver or receive a get.

(Bet Din of America)

B The Bet Din stamp

The requirements are:

- all converts must be immersed in a bath of rainwater (mikveh)
- male converts must be circumcised by a mohel (Brit Milah)
- the convert must believe that the Torah is God-given and that the 613 commandments contained within it must be obeyed (hamitzvot).

The rabbi who sponsored the convert has to provide the Bet Din with a report of the convert's progress one year after the ritual conversion.

The resolution of civil disputes

The Bet Din acts as an arbitrator when there are civil disputes over matters such as property or business disputes. In the UK the Bet Din's arbitration in such disputes is recognised by the Arbitration Act (1996) and is therefore legally binding.

The resolution of religious disputes

Arbitration over religious disputes is not legally binding under UK law but will be recognised by the Jewish community. Such matters could include issues related to the bringing up of children. It also includes the certification of mohelin as circumcision specialists, that is, people who are able to perform circumcision.

Kosher certification

The Bet Din provides certification to prove that a restaurant or food store is selling genuine kosher food (heschersher) or that animals are slaughtered according to the Jewish dietary laws (shochetim).

Medical ethics

The Bet Din may be called upon to assist Jewish patients and their relatives with any questions, which may arise related to medical ethics. These questions could be related to treatment or end of life issues such as abortion and euthanasia. The decisions related to medical ethics will depend very much on the branch of Judaism to which the Bet Din belongs. For example, the Orthodox position on abortion is different from that of Reform Jews who are more liberal in their approach to the practice.

∞ links

For more information about the role of the mohel see 5.4, pages 102–103.

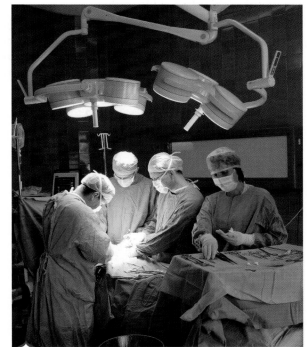

C *Jews need guidance to make decisions related to medical ethics*

Activities

1 Explain how the Bet Din supports the personal lifestyle of a Jew.
2 Explain what is required for conversion to Judaism.
3 'The Bet Din makes it easier for Jews to keep Jewish laws in the 21st century.' Do you agree? Give reasons for your opinion, showing that you have thought about more than one point of view.

Summary

You should now be able to explain the influence of the Bet Din on the personal lifestyle of a Jew.

AQA **Examiner's tip**

In your examination you need to be able to explain the function of the Bet Din in the 21st century.

4.10 Keeping a Jewish lifestyle in the 21st century

■ Is it possible for Jews to keep the Jewish laws in the 21st century?

Jews have to face many challenges related to their personal lifestyle in the 21st century. Some of the challenges that they have to face include the following:

■ Non-Jews arguing that many of the Jewish practices are impractical or outdated in the 21st century. For example, they may argue that the dietary laws were relevant to people living in the desert but because of refrigeration there are no longer health risks when combining milk and meat.

Beliefs and teachings

If a man lies with a man as one lies with a woman, both of them have done what is detestable. They must be put to death; their blood will be on their own heads.

Leviticus 20:13

■ Some of the punishments required by the Torah and Talmud would seem barbaric to people living in the UK, for example, the punishment required for homosexuality and adultery of death by stoning. Yet neither of these sexual practices is illegal under UK law and the country no longer has a death penalty.

■ Living in a non-Jewish country or community makes it harder to keep the Jewish laws, for example finding kosher food or keeping the Shabbat is difficult.

A committed Jew would agree that keeping the Jewish laws in the 21st century is difficult but not impossible. They would argue that the effort involved in keeping a Jewish personal lifestyle is another way in which devotion and obedience to God can be shown.

A *Driving is forbidden on Shabbat*

■ Are Jewish laws outdated in the 21st century?

Deciding whether or not Jewish laws are outdated in the 21st century depends very much on the interpretation of the Halakhah. For example, there are many laws that have had to change as they were based on practices performed in the Temple, and as the Temple was destroyed in 70 CE they can no longer be performed. For example, it is not possible for Jews to offer animal sacrifices to God as the Torah forbids such sacrifices outside the Temple.

In the absence of the Temple, Halakhic courts are not allowed to administer the death penalty so the attitude to homosexuality and adultery has changed. Orthodox Jews continue to consider homosexual relationships to be wrong but some branches of Reform Judaism place emphasis on the loving relationship between two people. Some

Objectives

Evaluate whether or not it is possible for Jews to keep the Jewish laws in their personal lifestyle in the 21st century.

∞ links

For more information about the sources of Jewish law, see Chapter 1, pages 8–13.

∞ links

Remind yourself of the dietary restrictions (pages 82–83), the problems of keeping the Shabbat observances (pages 78–79) and orthodox dress (pages 84-87) in this chapter.

Reform Jews known as Reconstructionist Jews will permit homosexuals to be rabbis and will marry gay couples in religious services.

Jews are not allowed to take ideas from other religions and cultures and include them within Judaism. However, Jews are allowed to do things that are similar to the culture of the region in which they live so long as it does not change Jewish practice. This is central to the diversity of opinion between the Orthodox and Reform traditions. Orthodox Jews argue that they have not changed Judaism even though they live alongside other cultures, but the Reform tradition has done so, by allowing changes in personal lifestyle. Within the different branches of the Reform movement there is diversity of opinion as to how the laws should be interpreted in the 21st century. They accept the binding nature of Halakhah but argue that Judaism is a religion that changes according to developments in the world in which they live. However the Reform movement does believe that Jews should live by the values and ethics of Judaism in their personal lives, and continue some of the practices and culture. Two examples that demonstrate how Jews are applying the Halakhah to modern situations that affect their personal lifestyle are the position of women and the use of contraception.

B *Jewish women must be modestly dressed*

The position of women

The original Jewish law on divorce did not require the wife to consent to the divorce. The changing status of women has resulted in the current situation in which both the man and woman have to give their consent to the divorce in the Orthodox tradition. Within Reform Judaism, women are able to obtain a get without their husband's consent.

Contraception

A married Jewish couple has to decide whether or not they can use modern methods of contraception. The rule related to birth control is that it is allowed so long as the sperm is not harmed. This means that most Jews are able to use the contraceptive pill but not a spermicidal jelly.

Discussion activity

With a partner, in a group or as a whole class discuss whether the fact that the Orthodox Jewish dress code allows women to wear modern dress so long as the skirt is not too short or the top too revealing means that they can wear the latest fashions.

∞ links

Read more about the status of women in Judaism on pages 118–119.

Activities

1 Explain why the destruction of the Temple in Jerusalem in 70 CE has made it difficult for Jews to keep some of the laws found in the Torah and Talmud.

2 Explain how the Jewish laws on divorce have changed in recent years.

3 Explain what would influence a Jew's choice of contraceptive.

4 'It is not possible for a Jew to live in the UK and still retain a Jewish personal lifestyle.' Do you agree? Give reasons for your answer, showing that you have thought about more than one point of view.

AQA Examiner's tip

Think of the actions a Jew living in the 21st century would consider to be against the law of God.

Summary

You should now be able to evaluate whether or not Jews can keep the Jewish laws in their personal lifestyle in the 21st century.

4

Personal lifestyle – summary

For the examination you should be able to:

✔ explain the Jewish dietary laws including the differences between food that is kosher and food that is trefah and the separation of milk and meat

✔ explain Shabbat observance as a day of rest

✔ explain the purpose and use of the mezuzah

✔ explain the Jewish attitude to wearing the kippah and orthodox dress

✔ explain the work of the Bet Din

✔ discuss the importance of the different Jewish views on dietary laws and dress.

Sample answer

1   Write an answer to the following exam question:

'It is not possible for Jews to keep holy the Sabbath Day in modern society.' Do you agree? Give reasons for your answer, showing you have thought about more than one point of view. *(6 marks)*

2   Read the following sample answer:

> I agree that it is difficult for Jews to keep holy the Sabbath Day when they live in non-Jewish communities. For example they may be living at a distance from the synagogue and yet they are not supposed to walk to the synagogue on the Sabbath. Also the Jewish Sabbath begins at different times throughout the year and they may be expected to work by their employer even though it is after sunset. It is not impossible for them to still keep the Sabbath day holy as they can rest, avoid activities believed to be work and read the Torah. For Jews living in Israel it will not be a problem as they will have a local synagogue, the Sabbath will start at the same time for everyone and everyone will be allowed to stop work at sunset.

3   With a partner discuss the sample answer. Do you think that there are other things that the student could have included in the answer?

4   What mark would you give this answer out of six? Look at the mark scheme in the Introduction on page 7 (A02). What are the reasons for the mark you have given?

AQA Examination-style questions

1 Look at the photograph below and answer the following questions below.

(a) Give two examples of food that is trefah in Judaism and explain why each one is trefah. *(4 marks)*

(b) Explain what is meant by kosher food. *(4 marks)*

(c) 'A mezuzah is an important symbol in a Jewish home.' Do you agree? Give reasons for your answer, showing you have thought about more than one point of view. *(6 marks)*

(d) Explain, using an example, how a Bet Din can support the personal lifestyle of a Jew. *(4 marks)*

(e) 'Jews can wear what they want.' Do you agree? Give reasons for your answer, showing you have thought about more than one point of view. *(6 marks)*

 Remember when you are asked 'Do you agree' with a statement, you must show what you think and the reasons why other people might take a different view. If your answer is one sided, you can only achieve a maximum of four marks. If you make no comment about religious belief or practice, you will achieve no more than three marks.

 You will be given a choice of two 24 mark questions in Section B of your exam. The parts of these questions will require longer answers so you may find it useful to plan your answers.

5.1 The importance of the family

■ The Fifth Commandment

The Fifth Commandment is:

> 66 *Honour your father and your mother, so that you may live long in the land the Lord your God is giving you.* 99
>
> *Exodus 20:12*

This commandment is one of the key teachings that shows the importance of the family in Jewish thought. Although there is not a similar commandment that instructs parents to respect their children if Jewish parents are following the faith as God intends, there would be no question that they would love, respect and care for their children anyway. Importantly, this love, respect and care extends to bringing children up within the Jewish faith and nurturing not only their physical development but also their spiritual development. This commandment emphasises this vital role of parents but also extends to older Jews who are expected to show respect to their own increasingly elderly parents whose needs are different.

For thousands of years, the Jewish family has been all inclusive – it extends to grandparents, grandchildren, cousins, aunts and uncles. However, with the growth of divorce rates and the greater geographical family spread in modern times, the togetherness and stability of Jewish families is coming under greater pressure. This is a challenge to those who want to retain the traditional extended family unit, along with the benefits it brings to the individual members and to the faith.

Activities

1 Make a note of the Fifth Commandment from Exodus 20:12.
2 What do you think 'honour your father and mother' means to:
   a a 3 year old
   b a 15 year old
   c a 50 year old?
3 How do you think the Jewish extended family unit can be maintained?

■ The home

There are two main centres of Jewish life: the synagogue and the home. Both inspire a sense of community, which provides security and trust. Their crucial role in Jewish life has been recognised for thousands of years. Even if a Jewish person can manage without a home, it is thought that Jewish culture and the preservation of the Jewish way of life cannot. It is mainly in the home that these are cherished, practised and passed on to future generations.

Objectives

Understand the importance of the family in Jewish thought.

Evaluate the strength of the family unit.

AQA Examiner's tip

Important quotations such as this one should be memorised and used in your exam if you get a chance.

A *An extended family shares a duty to observe their faith*

Discussion activity

With a partner, discuss whether honouring parents is good advice. What problems may dishonouring them bring? Be prepared to share your ideas with others.

Beliefs and teachings

God blessed them and said to them, 'Be fruitful and increase in number; fill the earth and subdue it'.

Genesis 1:28

Traditionally, the mother and father have distinct roles in the home and although in society in general, the roles of men and women are changing, great efforts are being made, especially in Orthodox Judaism, to ensure they remain.

The Jewish father should:

- provide financial and religious support for his family
- study the Torah and ensure that his sons and daughters do so as well.

The Jewish mother should:

- ensure that the home is a kosher home
- prepare the home for Shabbat and other festivals in which the home has a focus
- teach her daughters of their future role as wives and mothers, equipping them with the knowledge to carry it out successfully.

In some homes these roles are shared and the overall responsibility of parenthood is seen as the responsibility of both the father and the mother.

Simon and Mary

Simon has been married to Mary for 19 years. He works as an accountant for a large retail company. They both attend a Reform synagogue with their children on most Saturdays and especially to celebrate festivals. Their three children all attend the same Jewish secondary school, which happens to be the same school where Mary works as a teacher of mathematics. She had given up her career to support their children, but once they had all started secondary school she thought she should return to work rather than staying at home. Simon was a little worried that if his wife took on a full-time job, they would not be able to properly support the needs of their family but although Mary misses the fellowship of the Jewish women she met socially at the synagogue and elsewhere, she feels that she can combine the roles as wife, mother and teacher successfully. Simon has had to admit that she is right and that his fears were ungrounded because their home life still reflects and supports their faith, and in helping out around the house, both he and their children are learning valuable skills. The fact that Mary teaches at a Jewish school that closes early on winter Friday afternoons ensures that she can still perform her duties on Shabbat.

Case study

■ Children

It is expected that a Jewish married couple will have children. This is an expectation that comes from Genesis 1:28 (opposite).

Short of any act that could be interpreted as adultery (which would break the commandment in Exodus 20:14) or could harm the biological and religious identity of a child, a Jewish couple are allowed to use modern advances in fertility treatment if the wife cannot conceive naturally. Many Jews see such advances in medical technology as the work of God in enabling his command in Genesis to be met. The key point though is that a Jewish home is seen as incomplete without children, so a married couple choosing not to be parents is discouraged.

Activities

4 Write down your thoughts about the roles of the father and mother.

5 Read the case study. Do you think Simon and Mary are right to share their roles now she has returned to work? Explain your thoughts.

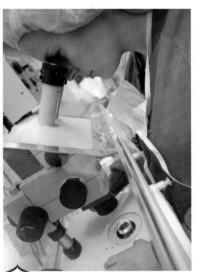

B *Jews are allowed to use fertility treatment to have children*

Activities

6 Why do you think Jewish married couples are expected to have children?

7 'Medical technology should have no part to play in the conception of a baby.' What do you think? Explain your opinion.

Summary

You should now understand more about the importance of the family unit in Judaism and have evaluated its strength.

5.2 The contribution of the synagogue to family life

■ The contribution to religious life

The home and the synagogue are the two focal points of Jewish life and religious observance. The synagogue contributes to religious life by offering opportunities to take part in structured worship, to participate in festivals and to hold ceremonies to mark rites of passage. It allows Jews within a community to meet together in fellowship and discuss matters of faith with faith leaders or other Jews.

Families are encouraged to worship together in a synagogue, although in Orthodox synagogues men sit separately from their wives and young children. Despite this separation, they are still all a part of the same worshipping congregation, praying together and hearing the same Torah readings.

■ The contribution of the synagogue to other parts of life

In addition to being used for worship, a synagogue is usually used as a community centre. There are often classrooms to teach young Jews about their faith and possibly how to read Hebrew. This is especially useful if the father does not feel confident enough to teach such things

A *The week in a typical synagogue*

Day	Services	Other events
Saturday	Shabbat 10.00 and 17.30	
Sunday	8.30, 15.00 and 18.30	Rabbi's surgery (10.00–11.30) Children's service (13.30–14.15) Fund-raising dinner for World Jewish Relief (20.00–late)
Monday	7.00, 14.00 and 18.45	Mother and baby group (11.00–13.30) Golden Wedding party (by invitation only) (20.00)
Tuesday	7.15, 14.15 and 18.30	Women's luncheon club (12.30) Young people's fellowship (19.30)
Wednesday	7.00, 14.00 and 18.45	Mother and baby group (11.00–13.30) Men's fellowship (20.00–22.00)
Thursday	7.15, 14.15 and 18.30	Kosher instruction and questions answered (9.30–10.30) Rabbi's surgery (16.00–17.30) Young people's fellowship (19.30)
Friday	7.00, 14.00 and 18.30	Friday night dinner (19.30)

Classes for young people (aged 8–15) between 17.30 and 19.30 Monday, Tuesday and Thursday

Classes for aged 16+ between 19.30 and 21.30 Monday and Thursday

Contact synagogue office for details of Brit Milah, Bar Mitzvah, Bat Mitzvah and weddings

Objectives

Understand the contribution the synagogue makes to family life.

Analyse and evaluate this contribution.

∞links

For more information on the synagogue, see Chapter 2.

Discussion activity 👥👥👥

'Keeping men and women separate in the synagogue does not affect Jewish belief in the importance of family life.' Discuss this statement with a partner or small group and then write down the points that are raised.

AQA Examiner's tip

The quality of your written communication will be assessed in your examination. Spelling specialist terms such as 'synagogue' correctly will help you to give evidence of high quality communication.

B *A synagogue is used for worship but also assists Jews in other parts of their life*

to his children. A synagogue also often has a hall, which is used for family and community celebrations such as weddings and Bar Mitzvahs, for meetings and possibly concerts. Specific groups for young people, mothers and babies and the elderly also meet in the synagogue, which helps to reinforce their identity as Jews and build the feeling of community.

A rabbi and other senior Jews are on hand to answer questions and help to resolve both religious and other issues encountered in living a life that is acceptable to God.

⊂⊃ links

The synagogue is used in many different ways. Look at 2.4 on pages 36–37 for more.

Case study

The Cohen family

The Cohen family live on an estate in a part of Manchester where there are several Jewish families. Mr Cohen owns a retail business and his wife, who has some training in accounts, helps him to keep the financial affairs of the business in order in addition to looking after their home. They have three children and Mr Cohen's elderly mother lives with them. She is keen for the whole family to keep the home a kosher home. In addition to using their local synagogue every Saturday morning for worship, they regularly spend evenings there. Their eldest son Joe is learning Hebrew because he hopes to become a rabbi later on in his life. His sister Rebekah does not share his enthusiasm for his faith but enjoys the company of her friends whom she meets at the youth club twice a week. She says she enjoys spending time with friends who have been brought up in a similar way to herself and share the same values. Although she doesn't call herself religious, she is keen to follow the traditional Jewish way of life, even though she doesn't always manage to do so. Ben, the youngest child in the family, is preparing for his Bar Mitzvah, which will be held in the synagogue in a couple of weeks. Although he is looking forward to it, he is nervous of reading to the rest of the congregation, especially in front of his friends. The party that will follow the ceremony will be a highlight!

A couple of years ago, Mr and Mrs Cohen were having problems in their marriage. Mr Cohen was spending too much time working and Mrs Cohen began to suspect that he was having an affair. As their rabbi is trained in marriage counselling, he managed to help them to resolve their differences. Consequently, Mrs Cohen was satisfied that her husband was not having an affair and Mr Cohen realised how his working hours were distressing his wife, so he has employed an assistant to take some of his workload. They are now living together happily again.

Hebrew lesson or football on television? Religion or football?

C

Activity

1 Explain what you think happens at a Rabbi's surgery?

Activity

4 Do young people need to choose between religion and other activities? What do you think? Explain your opinion.

Activities

2 Make up your own case study to show different ways a family uses a synagogue.

3 Should synagogues be used for non-worship purposes? Give your reasons.

Research activity 🔍

Do an internet search for the website of a synagogue in Britain, e.g. **www.singershill.com**. Try to discover how many different activities they offer.

Summary

You should now understand and be able to evaluate the contribution the synagogue makes to family life.

5.3   Birth

Introduction

The birth of a child is usually a happy event. This is especially so in the Jewish faith because having children is seen as fulfilling a duty to God. The instruction 'Be fruitful and increase in number' from Genesis 1:28 is used to encourage married Jews to have a family. This helps to maintain the faith, especially as conversion from another faith to Judaism is difficult.

Naming ceremony

Traditionally, a Jewish boy was named eight days after he was born at the ceremony of circumcision, whereas the birth of a girl was announced in the synagogue by her father. This took place about a month after she was born and the use of her name would introduce her formally to the Jewish community and to God. There was no obligation for the mother and her daughter to be present at the ceremony.

Nowadays, it is a little different. Boys are still circumcised after eight days but it is becoming more common for both boys and girls to be blessed, usually on the first Shabbat following the birth of the child. On this occasion, the father will be called forward to recite the aliyah (blessing of the Torah) and ask blessings for the health of the mother and their newly born baby. If the baby is a girl, she will be formally introduced by name at this point; if a boy, he is still named when circumcised. Jews living outside Israel are traditionally given a Hebrew name for use in religious matters such as the ketubah (wedding contract) and a secular name for daily use. This secular name is sometimes taken from the Tenakh and often from a family member. Ashkenazi Jews (Jews worldwide who are descended from German, Eastern European and Russian Jews) traditionally name a baby after a recently deceased relative, whereas Sefardi Jews (Jews historically descended from Spain, Portugal and North Africa) often use the name of a living relative.

Redemption of the first-born son

This ceremony, known in Hebrew as Pidyon Ha-Ben, is usually practised by Orthodox Jews. It takes its foundation from Numbers 18:14–16.

> #### Beliefs and teachings
>
> The first offspring of every womb, both man and animal, that is offered to the Lord is yours. But you must redeem every firstborn son ... When they are a month old, you must redeem them at the redemption price set at five shekels of silver ...
>
> **Numbers** 18:14–16

Objectives

Know and understand beliefs about birth and how Judaism marks the occasion.

Discussion activity

With a partner, discuss whether you think it is right for Jews to insist that having a family is a duty to God. Be prepared to share your ideas with others.

∞ links

For more information on circumcision, see 5.4.

Activities

1   Explain how the birth of a baby girl is announced in the synagogue.

2   Why do you think newly born Jews are often given a religious Hebrew name as well as a secular one?

A *Jews in America often use five silver dollars to redeem their first-born son*

There has never been a tradition of human sacrifice in Judaism but, traditionally, the first-born son was required to devote himself to service in the Temple. Nowadays this is not required, primarily because the Temple no longer exists, but many parents still choose to pay a small amount of money to a kohein (a descendent of the priestly family who would have served in the Temple) in order to maintain tradition by redeeming their son from Temple service. For redemption to be thought necessary, the boy must be born naturally (not by Caesarean section) and his mother must not have given birth to or miscarried another baby.

B   *A Jewish boy is often presented for redemption on a silver tray*

AQA *Examiner's tip*

Kohein can also be spelled kohen or cohen. Any of these spellings will be accepted in your examination.

The ceremony takes place 31 days after birth unless that falls on Shabbat or one of the festival days, such as Passover, when work and handling money is forbidden. In such an instance, it takes place on the next day. The kohein asks the father whether he wishes to give him the child or redeem him for five shekels. Once the father states he wishes to redeem him, he recites blessings and hands the kohein five silver coins. The kohein passes the coins over the baby's head while reciting:

66 *This is in place of that. This is excused on account of that. May it be that this son has entered into life, into Torah, and into fear of God. May it be God's will that just as he has entered into redemption, so may he enter into Torah, into marriage, and into good deeds.* 99

Extension activity

Explain the meaning of the words recited by the kohein. Do you think this puts a special responsibility on the redeemed first-born son when he grows up?

Activities

3   Explain why Jews believe that the first-born son needs to be redeemed.

4   Explain what happens during the ceremony of redemption of the first-born son.

Summary

You should now know and understand beliefs about birth and how Judaism marks the occasion.

5.4   Brit Milah – circumcision

■ The Brit Milah ceremony

When a baby boy is eight days old, he is presented for the **Brit Milah** ceremony during which he is circumcised. This is a requirement for any Jewish boy and will only be delayed if the baby is ill. The ceremony takes place either in the synagogue, the baby's home or a hospital, and is attended by family members and friends.

The process of circumcision is quite straightforward. The woman, chosen for the purpose, takes the baby from his mother and carries him on a cushion into a room where the invited men, including the father, have gathered. She hands him to the mohel who is trained to perform circumcisions and then leaves. He briefly places the baby boy onto an empty chair (Elijah's chair) to symbolise the presence of the spirit of the prophet Elijah, who is believed to be present at every circumcision. The baby is then placed on the knee of the sandek (companion of the child). Being chosen to be a sandek is considered an honour and the role is often given to the baby's grandfather or other respected member of the synagogue congregation. The mohel then effects the circumcision by removing the foreskin from the baby's penis – a simple operation that heals within a few days.

After the circumcision, the boy's father will say:

> ❝ *Blessed are you Lord our God, King of the Universe, who sanctified us with his Mitzvah and commanded us to enter my son into the covenant of Abraham.* ❞

And the others present respond:

> ❝ *As he has been entered into the covenant may he come to study the Torah, enter into a marriage worthy of the blessing and live a life of good deeds.* ❞

A Kiddush blessing is then said, wine is drunk with a few drops being given to the baby and he is formally named. The family and guests then enjoy a festive meal (Seudat Mitzvah) to celebrate the observance of this religious duty.

A   *Jewish boys are circumcised when they are eight days old*

Activities

1 Describe what happens during a Brit Milah ceremony.
2 Explain what you think each of the statements made by the father and the others present after the circumcision mean.

Extension activity

Find out other occasions when Jews use wine in religious observance.

■ What does circumcision mean?

The definition of a Jew is any person who has a Jewish mother. Circumcision is a mark of the baby's Jewish status because he has received his father's blessing and become religiously ready to be entered into membership of God's chosen race. Circumcision is a constant life-long reminder of this membership of God's chosen race.

The origins of circumcision come from the time of Abraham. God instructed him that he should be circumcised to confirm the covenant between God and himself and that this would be a requirement for all male Jews:

Beliefs and teachings

This is my covenant with you and your descendants after you, the covenant you are to keep: Every male among you shall be circumcised. You are to undergo circumcision, and it will be the sign of the covenant between me and you. For the generations to come every male among you who is eight days old must be circumcised... Any uncircumcised male, who has not been circumcised in the flesh, will be cut off from his people.

Genesis 17:10–12 and 14

B *Wine is drunk as part of the Kiddush blessing*

Thus circumcision is a way of initiation into the covenant required by both Orthodox and Reform Jews.

Activities

3 Explain why Jews consider circumcision to be so important.
4 'Just because Abraham was told circumcision was necessary doesn't mean it needs to be done in the 21st century.' Do you agree? Give reasons for your answer showing you have thought about more than one point of view.

Discussion activity

With a partner or small group discuss the statement 'It is unfair for parents to choose what religion a baby is going to follow.'

Summary

You should now know about the Brit Milah ceremony and understand its purpose and meaning.

∞ links

Read 1.8 on pages 22–23 for more about the Covenant with Abraham.

5.5　Bar Mitzvah

Coming of age

In Britain, there are various age restrictions. At the age of 15, a person can hold a firearms certificate (at the discretion of the police); they can have consensual sexual relations at 16 but have to be 18 to buy alcohol, tobacco or watch a film that has strong sexual content, extreme violence or bad language. They can get married at 16 with parental consent and 18 without; join the army at 16 years and 6 months; and vote in an election or go to war at 18. Below the age of 10 a child is legally considered too young to be charged with committing a crime.

Although Jews in Britain are happy to respect these age restrictions, for the purposes of their faith, boys are considered to have come of age as adults when they reach 13 and girls when they reach 12, because they believe that at these ages, young people become able to take responsibility for their own actions.

Bar Mitzvah

The literal meaning of **Bar Mitzvah** is 'son of the commandment' and refers to the coming of age of a Jewish boy. It is at the age of 13 that a boy is obliged to follow the commandments as if he were an adult. He becomes responsible for his own faith, replacing his father in this role. He also gains the right to take an active part in synagogue worship, even leading parts of it and is counted in the minimum number required to perform certain synagogue observances (minyan). These rights and obligations are granted to any Jewish boy on his 13th birthday whether or not he participates in a special ceremony. Strictly speaking, there is no need to have a ceremony to mark the coming of age; Bar Mitzvah ceremonies are not mentioned in the Torah or Talmud, although their use may be implied from a reference in Mishnah Brurah 225:6 to a Mitzvah feast.

The ceremony

At the basic level, Bar Mitzvah is the boy's first aliyah (blessing of the Torah). However, it has become more than that in many instances. On the first Shabbat following the boy's 13th birthday, he will often be called up to read from the Torah during the regular Shabbat service. This may be the whole scheduled reading including the traditional chant or just a part of it and is often recited from memory. He will wear a tallit for the first time in the synagogue and may also lead part of the service or some of the prayers and often make a short speech beginning with 'Today I am a man'. His father also recites a blessing, thanking God for bringing his son to maturity and declaring that he is now responsible for his own actions.

Preparations for Bar Mitzvah can take weeks to ensure that the blessing and reading are performed properly because errors will distract from the worship for the whole congregation. Many synagogues hold classes to help a boy prepare for his Bar Mitzvah and to ensure he knows sufficient about his faith to live the life God requires from him.

Objectives

Know and understand about the Bar Mitzvah ceremony.

Understand why Jews believe Bar Mitzvah is important.

Discussion activity

Spend two minutes discussing with a partner whether you agree with Jews that girls and boys are sufficiently responsible for keeping their faith at the ages of 12 and 13.

Key terms

Bar Mitzvah: celebration of a boy coming of age at 13. Literally 'son of the commandment'.

Beliefs and teachings

It is a Mitzvah (i.e. a good and obligatory deed) to make a meal on the day one's son becomes a Bar Mitzvah, just like the day of his wedding ... The reason for the meal is because he has now become an adult Jew who is now required to observe all the Mitzvoth (Commandments) of the Torah. This has the status of a Feast of Mitzvah. If, however, the meal is not held on the day he becomes 13 years, but is held on some day later, then the Bar Mitzvah should lecture on Torah teachings, and then the meal will have the status of a Feast of Mitzvah.

Mishnah Brurah 225:6

Activity

1. 'A Bar Mitzvah ceremony is pointless because a Jewish boy becomes a son of the commandments when 13 anyway.' Do you agree? Give reasons for your answer showing you have thought about more than one point of view.

Activities

2. Explain what happens during a Bar Mitzvah ceremony.
3. Write your own 'Today I am a man' speech that could be used during a Bar Mitzvah ceremony.

Today I am a man. I have responsibilities which I must keep. I have known the commandments since I was a young child. Now is the time for me to make sure I keep them. If I don't, I can only blame myself. Reading the Torah in the synagogue today was the scariest thing I have done but I think I got it right – I hope God agrees. With His help, I know my adult life is going to be good.

A

Traditionally, a small celebration followed a Bar Mitzvah and religious gifts such as books were given. Nowadays, Orthodox Jews often have a celebratory meal attended by at least one rabbi who may speak about the Torah, praise the Bar Mitzvah boy and encourage him to take his new responsibilities seriously. Other Orthodox Jews, along with most Reform Jews, hold an extravagant party in the boy's honour. Opponents of this believe that Bar Mitzvah is a serious religious occasion with a deep spiritual meaning, not an opportunity to spend money on a lavish party, which may live longer in the memory than the actual ceremony.

B   *A Bar Mitzvah boy reads from the Torah during the Shabbat service*

Activities

4. What do you think would be an appropriate Bar Mitzvah gift? Explain why.
5. In your opinion, do you think it is appropriate to have a party after a Bar Mitzvah ceremony? What do you think? Give reasons for your answer.

Summary

You should now know and understand about the Bar Mitzvah ceremony and why Jews believe Bar Mitzvah is important.

AQA   **Examiner's tip**

If asked to write about the ceremony, don't spend too much time writing about the party afterwards.

5.6 Bat Mitzvah and Bat Chayil

■ Bat Mitzvah

In a similar way to Bar Mitzvah, **Bat Mitzvah** means 'daughter of the commandments'. It has the same meaning – marking the moment when a girl becomes a full member of the faith, responsible for her actions and for keeping the commandments. Because girls mature at an earlier age than boys, Bat Mitzvah occurs a year earlier than Bar Mitzvah, when a girl has her 12th birthday but often, especially in Orthodox Judaism, it is not celebrated in a similar way.

As with Bar Mitzvah, no ceremony is needed for a girl to become Bat Mitzvah and it is only over the last 100 years that holding a ceremony has become increasingly popular in Reform Judaism to the extent that the celebrations are now very similar to Bar Mitzvah ceremonies. Many Reform Jews feel that because there is nothing forbidding holding a Bat Mitzvah celebration, there is no reason why they should not do so, provided their celebration does not break Jewish laws. Others consider it to be a matter of the girl's individual choice, although their family may seek to influence this choice. If she is proud of the fact she has come of age according to her faith, and it means something to her, a Bat Mitzvah ceremony seems appropriate. The ceremony may involve her reading or saying prayers in the synagogue as at a Bar Mitzvah. If, however, it is just to have a good time at the celebration or in the cause of equality, many Jews would express concern.

Because women do not take an active part in worship in Orthodox Judaism, they do not usually mark Bat Mitzvah with a religious ritual. Instead, they may perhaps enjoy a family meal at home and by giving small religious gifts. The girl may make a short speech to show her awareness of what Bat Mitzvah involves. If she wants to, she can choose to read from the Torah in the synagogue but this will only be in the presence of other women and not in the main part of the prayer hall.

The London School of Jewish Studies runs courses for Bat Mitzvah girls to spend time with their mothers so that they can both study their faith, the lives of prominent Jewish women, Jewish texts and just to spend some time sharing thoughts and joining together in discussion. The girl's future role in keeping a Jewish home is also emphasised. They also practise the making of challah bread for Shabbat observance, as some Jews believe that making challah bread is one of the new responsibilities for a Bat Mitzvah girl.

Objectives

Understand the meaning of Bat Mitzvah and Bat Chayil and the way they are observed.

Consider the differences between Bar Mitzvah and Bat Mitzvah.

Key terms

Bat Mitzvah: celebration of a girl coming of age at 12, in Reform Synagogues. Literally 'daughter of the commandment'.

Bat Chayil: celebration of a girl coming of age at 12, in Orthodox Synagogues. Literally 'daughter of valour'.

Discussion activity ●●●

Discuss with a partner, preferably of a different gender from yourself, whether you think it is right that a girl should become Bat Mitzvah a year before a boy becomes Bar Mitzvah.

A *Making challah bread is one of the new responsibilities for a Bat Mitzvah girl*

Activities

1. Explain what being Bat Mitzvah means to a 12-year-old Jewish girl.
2. Do you think a Jewish girl should have a religious ceremony to become Bat Mitzvah? Give reasons for your choice.
3. What do you think the London School of Jewish Studies should include in their Bat Mitzvah course? Explain why.
4. Can you think of any prominent Jewish women from the past or present who should be studied on such a course?

Bat Chayil

The literal meaning of **Bat Chayil** is 'daughter of valour'. Many synagogues offer a Bat Chayil course to girls soon after they have become Bat Mitzvah followed by a ceremony in the synagogue. Bat Chayil courses give groups of girls around 13 years old the opportunity to learn about their faith including their role in Shabbat and festivals, keeping a Jewish home, studying Jewish history and learning some prayers and blessings. The synagogue ceremony that follows the course focuses on the success of the girl's learning with displays of projects they have completed during it, and reciting of prayers and reading from the Torah, which they have learnt. This highlights the importance of continuing Jewish education even after Bat Mitzvah.

Examiner's tip

Remember that Bat Chayil comes after a girl has become Bat Mitzvah.

Research activity

Do an internet search to find more about what a Bat Chayil course might include.

Esther speaks about her faith

Esther is a Jewish girl who attends a Reform synagogue in North London. She speaks proudly about her faith:

'A couple of months before my 12th birthday, my parents sat me down and we had a serious chat about our faith. They allowed me to choose whether I wanted a ceremony for my Bat Mitzvah. They told me that it would not be considered as important as my brother Nathan's Bar Mitzvah, but that I could have a party afterwards anyway. I thought for a few days before I decided that I preferred to have a nice meal with the whole family invited instead. After all, whether I have a ceremony or not wouldn't matter; I will still be Bat Mitzvah whatever happens and I didn't want the party to make me lose sight of that fact. I did ask them to arrange a Bat Chayil course for me though and I start that next week. I still cherish the gifts I was given, a beautiful copy of the Tenakh from my parents and a storybook about great Jewish women and a beautifully decorated pushke for me to use to collect money for charity and remember those less fortunate than myself. I really do count myself lucky to have a faith.'

B *Esther is proud of her faith and that she is Bat Mitzvah, even though she didn't have a ceremony*

Case study

Activities

5 Script a conversation between Esther and her elder brother Nathan about whether she should have chosen to take part in a Bat Mitzvah ceremony.

6 Do you think a party would have made Esther lose sight of the importance of a Bat Mitzvah ceremony had she chosen to have one? Give reasons for your answer.

Extension activity

Write a case study of either a boy or girl who chose to have a religious ceremony to mark their Bar Mitzvah or Bat Mitzvah. Explain their thoughts about what happened and how they felt during the ceremony.

Summary

You should now understand the meaning of Bat Mitzvah and Bat Chayil and have considered the differences between Bat Mitzvah and Bar Mitzvah.

∞ links

See pages 104–105 for information on the Bar Mitzvah.

5.7 | Marriage

Betrothal (kiddushin)

There are several ways in which young Jews may find a partner to marry. Traditionally parents, often helped by a matchmaker, chose a partner for their son or daughter to marry. This is still practised by ultra Orthodox and some Orthodox Jews who believe that a matchmaker (shadchan) is actively working on God's behalf by pairing up people for **marriage**. The couple can be involved in deciding whether they will proceed to getting married although they are unlikely to go against the advice of the matchmaker because they believe they are being helped to find God's choice of husband or wife for them.

Nowadays, reform Jewish couples tend to choose each other, often with the help of the synagogue, which may hold functions for single Jews looking for a marriage partner or even a specialist Jewish dating agency. Some Jews believe that provided the match is well made, love will grow during a marriage and 'falling in love' does not have to happen before marriage.

Once the couple have decided to marry and parental approval has been obtained, the couple become betrothed (kiddushin). Kiddushin means 'sanctified' or 'set aside', so **betrothal** signifies that the couple are set aside for each other. In Jewish law, this has legal status and so can only be broken by death or divorce. Traditionally this agreement was announced at a special kiddushin ceremony a year before marriage, but today this ceremony is usually just before the actual wedding although the couple will still hope to be betrothed for around a year before getting married. The couple will not live together while betrothed and they are not allowed to have sexual relationships with each other (or anyone else). They do however make preparations for their life together.

In the synagogue, it is common for the husband to be involved in aliyah (Torah blessing) during the last Shabbat service before the wedding is due to take place, and then to formally announce his intention to marry. This is often followed by the congregation meeting to share food, drink and wine in celebration of the forthcoming event. The families of the couple usually share a celebration lunch with them. This is likely to be the last time the couple see each other before their wedding.

During betrothal, a wedding contract (ketubah) is drawn up, which formally lists the husband's obligations to his wife while they are married, sets out conditions of inheritance upon his death, on the support of children of the marriage, and how he will provide for his wife if they get divorced. Extra conditions can also be added if they both agree, including the wife's responsibilities to her husband.

Objectives

Know and understand what happens during a Jewish wedding.

Key terms

Marriage: a legal union between a man and a woman.

Betrothal: an engagement, traditionally 12 months before a Jewish wedding.

Discussion activity

'As parents know their children better than anybody, it makes sense for them to choose their marriage partner for them.' Discuss this statement with a partner and be prepared to share your ideas with others.

A *The ketubah is signed before the couple are married*

Activities

1. Do you think a 12-month betrothal is a good idea? Give your reasons.

2. Why do you think betrothed couples are not allowed to have a sexual relationship with each other?

3. What extra conditions would you like to add to a ketubah? Explain why.

The wedding ceremony

Jewish wedding ceremonies usually take place in the synagogue on any day except Shabbat. Traditionally, they took place outside under a canopy, called a chuppah, to symbolise the couple's future home. In many ceremonies today the synagogue will provide a chuppah indoors for the couple to stand under. A rabbi usually leads the ceremony, although this is not essential.

If the betrothal ceremony (kiddushin) was not performed when the couple became betrothed, it is performed before the actual wedding ceremony. The bride approaches and circles the groom. They then recite two blessings over wine, the first a standard blessing and the second related specifically to marriage. While exchanging rings, they declare, 'Behold, you are consecrated to me by this ring according to the Law of Moses and Israel.' The ketubah is then read and given to the bride (this may be done before the rings are exchanged), before the actual wedding ceremony takes place.

While the couple are standing beneath the chuppah, they recite seven wedding blessings along with the rabbi. At some point the rabbi will make a short speech about the couple before blessing them in front of the congregation. A song of seven blessings is usually sung towards the end of the service. The final act of the ceremony involves the groom breaking a glass (wrapped in paper or cloth for safety) under his heel, to symbolise the destruction of the Temple and to show regret that the wedding could not have taken place there. It is also a symbol of the fact that in life there is great happiness but also great sadness. It is also sometimes said that the smashing of the glass symbolises taking away the bride's virginity now they are married. After the glass has been smashed, the congregation shout 'mazel tof', which means good fortune.

B *A newly wed Jewish couple under a Chuppah*

Finally the newly married couple get to spend a few minutes alone in a private room to symbolise their new status as husband and wife. This is called yikhud (seclusion).

A joyous celebration follows, usually involving music or dancing. Many Reform Jews spend some time away together on honeymoon while Orthodox Jews tend to stay at home and visit friends and family as honoured guests for a meal before returning to their new home.

Extension activity

Draft a ketubah listing a husband's obligations to his wife, inheritance, support of children and provision for divorce. Include extra conditions if you feel you need to.

AQA Examiner's tip

You are only expected to know Hebrew words which are in the specification. However, if you know other Hebrew terms you can use them.

Activities

4 Draft an invitation to a Jewish wedding. Include some details of what will happen during and after the ceremony.

5 What is the symbolic meaning of the breaking of a glass?

6 Would you prefer to go on honeymoon or spend a week visiting friends and family? Which of these would be a better start to the marriage? Explain your reasons.

Summary

You should now know and understand about betrothal and marriage in Judaism.

5.8 The significance of marriage

Introduction

Marriage is regarded as very important in Judaism and it is seen as a natural part of a person's life. There is no religious merit in remaining unmarried. The chief reason for its importance is because it provides a stable home environment to bring up a family. Jews believe that in order to be parents, the man and woman should be married – sex outside marriage is forbidden. The home and family, along with the synagogue community, is considered to be the centre of religious life.

Who should a Jew marry?

The first requirement for a Jew is that they should marry a fellow Jew. There are many reasons for this but the main one is that marrying within the faith contributes to keeping the faith alive. Children are then brought up in a Jewish household that encourages them to follow the faith.

A person is regarded as being Jewish if their mother is Jewish. If a Jewish woman marries a non-Jewish man, their children will be considered to be Jewish. However, their non-Jewish father is unlikely to be able to fulfil his responsibility to bring up his children in a Jewish fashion, teaching them about Jewish beliefs and practices, and he will not be permitted to take any active part in synagogue services in the event that he chooses or is allowed to attend for the sake of his children. A Jewish male relative from the mother's side of the family could fulfil this role on behalf of the father.

The Torah lays down strict rules prohibiting marriage between certain family members including close blood relatives, a divorced person whose divorce is invalid in Jewish law and children of an ex-spouse (Leviticus 18).

> If I agree to marry you, I insist we bring up our children as Jews in a Jewish home.

> No problem, I wouldn't want it to be any other way. We can include it in the ketubah.

A

Activity

1   Explain why it is considered important for a Jew to marry a fellow Jew.

Why do Jews marry?

The requirement for Jewish couples to have children comes primarily from the instruction to be fruitful and increase in number from Genesis 1:28. Whilst this is important, it is not the only reason why Jewish people believe marriage is necessary. Companionship, love (which grows throughout the marriage) and intimacy are also important human needs that marriage helps to fulfil. The Torah tells Jews that, having created Adam, God recognised the need for him to have the company of a partner:

Activities

2   Explain why it would be difficult for a non-Jewish father to raise children into the Jewish way of life.

3   'A Jewish male relative from the mother's side of the family could take charge of Jewish education on behalf of the father.' What do you think? Explain your opinion.

Beliefs and teachings

It is not good for the man to be alone. I will make a helper suitable for him.

Genesis 2:18

The law recognises the importance of marriage in Deuteronomy 24:5:

Beliefs and teachings

If a man has recently married, he must not be sent to war or have any other duty laid on him. For one year, he is to be free to stay at home and bring happiness to the wife he has married.

Deuteronomy 24:5

Research activity

Divorce is possible in Judaism although it is not very common. Try to find out more about divorce in Judaism. Start your search at www.jewfaq.org/divorce.htm

In order for a husband and wife to fulfil their traditional roles, the husband is responsible for providing his wife with sufficient food and clothing for herself and her family. He must also ensure the marriage fulfils the wife's right to sexual relationships (Exodus 21:10). He does not have a similar right so he cannot force her to satisfy his sexual desires, nor can he seek a sexual relationship outside marriage because adultery is forbidden.

For her part, the wife is responsible for the home. It is she who begins the weekly Shabbat ceremony in the home by lighting the Shabbat candles. This is a small part of her main role, which has traditionally been to ensure the home is fit to bring up her family and allow them all to follow their faith. This includes keeping the rules of Kashrut by providing food that is kosher.

While Orthodox Jewish women tend to be happy to fulfil this role, the obligation on Reform Jewish women to do the same has been relaxed in many cases in the name of equality. However, this does not alter the fact that any Jewish couple is expected to have children and bring them up in an environment where their faith is introduced and nurtured.

B   *Jewish children should be brought up to keep the laws of Kashrut*

Extension activity

Apart from what it says above in Deuteronomy, how else do you think people can be helped during their first year of marriage? Explain the reasons for your ideas.

Activities

4   Companionship, love and intimacy are important human needs that marriage helps to fulfil? Do you agree? Give reasons for your answer showing that you have thought about more than one point of view.

5   Explain the different roles of a husband and wife. Do you think that these different roles should exist or should it be left to the couple to decide? Explain your reasons.

AQA *Examiner's tip*

As there are wide differences in interpretation between and within Jewish groups, it helps to use such terms as 'some', 'many', 'most' to show this difference, e.g. most Orthodox Jews …, some Reform Jews …, rather than implying that all Jews think the same.

Summary

You should now know and understand what Jews believe the purpose of marriage to be and have analysed and considered these beliefs.

5.9 Death and mourning

Life and death

Jews value life but recognise that death is a natural ending to life and part of God's plan that cannot be avoided. The 613 mitzvoth (the rules that tell them what they should and shouldn't do) apart from those associated with murder, idolatry, incest and adultery can be broken if the intention is to save life. Therefore, a dying person can be driven to hospital and treated on the Shabbat without any fear of breaking the law, and sick people are not expected to fast during Yom Kippur. However, because life is so valuable, nothing to bring death more quickly (e.g. suicide or euthanasia) is permitted, although life shouldn't be prolonged artificially in cases where death is certain and imminent.

It is expected that no Jew will die alone. If their death is imminent, their family will try to visit them, ensuring someone stays with them until they die. It is considered to be an act of great kindness to be with a person at the moment of their death and to ensure that their eyes are closed after they have died. If possible, the dying person will make a final confession and recite the Shema just before they die. In Orthodox Judaism, those present (and others), on first hearing of the death of a loved one, will traditionally follow the example of Jacob by making a small tear in their clothes. For a close family member, the tear is made over the heart and for others on the right-hand side of the chest:

Objectives

Know and understand Jewish practices associated with death and mourning.

Key terms

Mourning: a period of time spent remembering a person who has died.

> ### Beliefs and teachings
>
> Then Jacob tore his clothes, put on sackcloth and mourned his son for many days.
>
> **Genesis** 37:34

> ### Beliefs and teachings
>
> Blessed are You, Lord, our God, King of the universe, the True Judge.

Reform Jews are more likely to cut a neck tie or wear a torn black ribbon. They make a blessing to God (see Beliefs and teachings, right) referring to him as the true judge to show their acceptance of God taking the person's life.

Activities

1. Give examples to show that Jews consider life to be very important.
2. Explain what a Jewish family does before and after a family member dies.

A Jews light a Yahrzeit candle on the anniversary of a death

Mourning

To allow full expression of **mourning** but also to gradually help a mourner to get back to normal life, times for mourning are clearly set out for Jews to follow. The most intense mourning occurs between the time of death and burial.

links

For information on burial practices, see 5.10.

At this time, mourners from the deceased's close family are called 'immediate mourners'. They are not required to obey the positive mitzvot (those that tell them what they should do, rather than what they mustn't do), but are left alone to allow them full expression of their grief.

Once the burial has taken place, the 'immediate mourners' are sometimes called 'prolonged mourners'. A close friend or relative prepares a meal of eggs (new life) and bread for the mourners. This is called a meal of condolence and marks the end of the immediate period of care for the deceased.

The next seven days are spent in intense mourning (shiva). The mourners stay at home and sit on low stools or the floor instead of chairs, do not wear leather shoes, shave or cut their hair, wear cosmetics or work. They also do not do things for comfort or pleasure, such as bathing, having sex, putting on fresh clothing or studying Torah (except that related to mourning and grief). They wear the clothes that they tore at the time of learning of the death or at the funeral. Mirrors in the house are covered so they do not focus on their appearance. Three times a day, prayer services are held in the home where the shiva is held, with friends, neighbours and relatives making up the minyan (ten people required for certain prayers). During this time, the mourners' kaddish is recited to praise God and pray for the coming age of eternal peace. It begins:

'May His great Name grow exalted and sanctified in the world that He created as He willed.'

Once shiva has finished, the period of lesser mourning begins. This ends 30 days after the person's death. During this time, normal life resumes but mourners do not attend parties, listen to music or shave or cut their hair. Male mourners say the mourners' kaddish in the synagogue daily.

The final period of mourning is observed only for a parent. Mourners avoid celebrations such as parties for 11 months and the male mourners continue to say the mourners' kaddish every day. Once the final period of mourning is over, formal mourning stops, although on each anniversary of the death (Yahrzeit), sons recite the mourners' kaddish, if possible make an aliyah (Torah blessing) and light a Yahrzeit candle, which burns for 24 hours.

Activity

3   Draw a timeline divided into months from 0 to 12 months. On this timeline, mark on immediate, prolonged, lesser and final mourning. For each, draw a small symbol to help remind you of what they are.

Discussion activity

Spend three minutes discussing with a partner whether you think seven days' intense mourning is a good idea. Try to think of some reasons for your opinions and be prepared to share them with others.

Research activity

Look at www.jewfaq.org/prayer/kaddish.htm for the words of the mourners' kaddish in Hebrew and English.

AQA   Examiner's tip

There is a lot of detail on these pages. You will not be expected to give so much detail in your exam.

Activities

4   Which of the four stages of mourning do you think is most important? Give your reasons.

5   Do you agree that structuring mourning in this way is helpful? Give your reasons.

6   'Lighting a Yahrzeit candle is a good way of remembering a loved one.' Do you agree? Give reasons for your answer showing that you have thought about more than one point of view. Refer to Judaism in your answer.

Summary

You should now know and understand Jewish attitudes associated with death and mourning.

B   *Jews make a tear in their clothing as a sign of mourning for their loved ones who have died*

5.10 The funeral and beliefs about the afterlife

Preparation of the body

Jews are required to bury bodies rather than cremating them. This should happen as soon after death as possible, usually within 24 hours, although some Reform Jewish funerals are delayed to allow friends and family to attend. While the body is awaiting burial, someone stays with it and candles are lit beside it. Many Jewish communities have an organisation called Chevra Kaddisha to care for the body and prepare it for burial. These are well-known Jews from the community, which means that the body is looked after and prepared for burial by people the deceased knew and not strangers. Family members may also choose to be involved.

The body is washed carefully, men by men and women by women. It is then wrapped in a plain linen shroud and in a tallit (in the case of men usually). One of the corner fringes (tzitzit) is removed from the tallit to signify that it will no longer be used for prayer in life. The body is then placed in a simple coffin to show that in death there is equality between the rich and poor because they are treated the same. The coffin is then sealed.

The funeral

Funerals do not take place in a synagogue because a synagogue is regarded as a place of the living. The body is transported direct to the cemetery for burial. During the short service, psalms are read, prayers are said and a rabbi says a few words about the deceased person. The coffin is then lowered into the ground and the mourners shovel earth onto the top of the coffin. After offering words of comfort to the mourners, everybody washes their hands before leaving the cemetery to symbolise leaving death behind.

The tombstone

It is a requirement in Jewish law that a tombstone is erected on the grave so the person is not forgotten. Some Jews either keep the tombstone veiled or delay erecting it until the end of the 12-month mourning period. They believe that during this period, no headstone is necessary because the deceased will not be forgotten. There is often a small ceremony to mark the unveiling or erection of the tombstone. Flowers are not used to remember the dead, but visitors may place a small stone on a grave.

Beliefs about life after death

There is little teaching in Jewish holy books about life after death. The emphasis is on living correctly with the implication that correct living will influence what happens after death. Jews are however convinced that death is not the end.

Activities

1 Explain how a body is prepared for burial.

2 Why do you think a tallit is used in dressing the body?

⚭ links

See 5.9 for mourning customs that follow the funeral.

Discussion activity

1 Traditionally, Jews have always buried their dead, although nowadays some Reform Jews are cremated. With a partner, discuss which practice you think is best. You may want to consider life after death in your discussions.

A Visitors to graves often place a small stone on them to mark their visit

Holy books give bits of information about life after death, which, when put together, give us a more complete picture. However, there can be little certainty that it is accurate. For this reason, Orthodox and Reform Jews do not agree.

Early teachings in the Torah refer to rejoining one's ancestors upon death. The phrase used to describe this as 'gathered to his people'. However, over time this belief appeared to change.

■ Sheol

Sheol is mentioned several times in the Tenakh, including in the Torah. It is described as a shadowy place of darkness and silence where all souls exist without consciousness. In later parts of the Tenakh, the idea that Sheol is a temporary state develops. From this the idea that the soul is immortal arises.

■ Resurrection

The prophet Daniel, whose prophecies were probably written down during the 2nd century BCE long after his death, looks forward to a time of resurrection.

The Talmud gives further ideas about resurrection but there are many Jews today, mainly from the Reform tradition, who reject resurrection.

■ Judgement

Reform Jews have no specific official belief about judgement and the world to come and there is much debate about who qualifies to go to Gan Eden (heaven) and Gehinnom (hell), and whether these are two states of consciousness or actual physical or spiritual places. Moses Maimonides, the 12th-century Jewish philosopher, made it clear that Gan Eden is not exclusively for Jews when he wrote:

> 66 *the pious of all nations of the world have a portion in the world to come.* 99

■ The Messianic Age

Some Jews believe that a messiah will come to lead a golden Messianic Age when the righteous dead will resurrect and live in a time of peace in a restored Israel. At this time, the Temple will be rebuilt in Jerusalem. Many Reform Jews also look forward to this time but reject the idea of an individual messiah.

Activity

3 How do you think believing in life after death affects the everyday life of a typical Jewish person? Give examples.

Summary

You should now know and understand about Jewish funeral customs and ideas about life after death and have evaluated the link between living and life after death.

> 66 *What can we know of death, we who cannot understand life?'* 99
>
> *Jewish prayer*

Discussion activity 👤👤👤

2 With a partner or small group discuss what you believe about life after death. Do you have good evidence for what you believe?

Beliefs and teachings

Multitudes who sleep in the dust of the earth will awake: some to everlasting life, others to shame and everlasting contempt.

Daniel 12:2

AQA Examiner's tip

If you are asked about Jewish beliefs about life after death, you may include the fact that there is little specific teaching, which means that Orthodox and Reform Jews disagree. This will be seen as evidence of good understanding.

Research activity 🔍

Look at *Genesis* 35:29; *Job* 10:21–22 and *Daniel* 12:2–3 to identify how beliefs about life after death changed.

Extension activity

Explain what you think about the belief in a Messianic Age when the righteous dead will resurrect and live in a restored Israel.

5

Family life – summary

For the examination, you should now be able to:

✔ show understanding of Jewish views on relationships and family life and relate them to:

– the importance of the family

– the contribution of the synagogue to family life

– ceremonies associated with birth

– Brit Milah

– Bar/Bat Mitzvah

– Bat Chayil

– marriage ceremonies and their significance

– ceremonies associated with mourning and death

✔ apply relevant Jewish teachings to each topic

✔ discuss topics from different points of view, including Jewish ones.

Sample answer

1 Write an answer to the following examination question.

'Describe a Jewish wedding ceremony.' *(6 marks)*

2 Read the following answer.

> Jews marry in synagogues but not on Shabbat. They stand under a chuppah for the ceremony, which is led by a rabbi. They will probably have a betrothal ceremony first even though they have been betrothed for a year. They say some blessings and drink some wine. The man gives the woman a ring while saying some words. They read the marriage contract before saying some more words and blessings. It finishes with the man smashing a glass while people shout good luck to him.

3 With a partner, discuss the sample answer. Do you think that there are other things that the student could have included in the answer?

4 What mark would you give this answer out of six? Look at the mark scheme in the Introduction on page 7 (AO1). What are the reasons for the mark you have given?

AQA Examination-style questions

1   Look at the photograph below and answer the following questions

(a)   Explain what happens at a Bar Mitzvah.   *(4 marks)*

 As there are four marks available, you must give some details including why Jews do what they do.

(b)   Explain **two** ways in which a Bar Mitzvah ceremony is different from a Bat Mitzvah ceremony.   *(4 marks)*

 You will earn one mark for **each** of the two ways you give (provided they are correct) and one mark for writing extra detail or explaining **each** one, giving four marks in total.

(c)   'Religious ceremonies are more for the family than the individual.' Do you agree? Give reasons for your answer, showing that you have thought about more than one point of view. Refer to Judaism in your answer.   *(6 marks)*

 Before you start writing, think carefully. You have to provide reasons, including ones taken from Judaism for each of two different points of view and explain how they relate to the quotation.

6.1 The role and status of women in Judaism

Role and status

Objectives

Understand the difference between status and roles.

Begin to understand and evaluate the roles and status of women in Judaism.

There is a great deal of misunderstanding about the difference between a person's **role** and a person's **status**. Their role is what they do – the actions they perform or are expected to perform. Their status is the importance other people attach to their role while they are performing it. For instance, the role of your teacher is to lead your learning by providing opportunities for you to advance. Teachers have knowledge, skills and experience that they use to help you to do this. If you are fortunate enough to have a teaching assistant in your lesson, their role is to assist you and your teacher to ensure that you are able to take the opportunities the teacher offers you in your learning. Their roles are different.

Key terms

Role: the actions a person performs; what they do.

Status: how important a person's role makes them in other people's estimation.

These different roles give teachers and teaching assistants different status in the classroom. Your teacher leads the learning and has overall responsibility for your progress. The teaching assistant has a vital role in assisting this process under the guidance of the teacher. However, the teacher's increased status does not make them a better person or give them more rights than the teaching assistant. They get paid more to recognise their greater responsibility in ensuring you learn as much as possible, but in other respects, as human beings in society outside the school, they each have the same rights and status.

The headteacher of course has a different role in ensuring that your school is led and managed in such a way that you can learn and your teachers can teach effectively. That extra responsibility gives your head teacher greater status in school but in society she or he has just the same rights and status in society as anybody else. Status is only of importance in situations where the roles that provide that status apply.

Wealthy people may be seen to have greater status than poorer people. But does that mean they get served first in a shop if there is a queue? Are they allowed to drive more quickly than poorer people just because they may have a more powerful and expensive car? The answer to these questions is no – their perceived status brought about by their wealth does not mean they are or should be treated differently from poorer people – all should be treated with respect regardless of status.

 We are all subject to the same laws, whatever our role or status

Extension activity

Make a list of groups of people in your school, e.g. teachers and teaching assistants, in order of what you think their status is within the school. Is this only determined by their roles?

AQA   Examiner's tip

If asked to explain the difference between two words, don't just define both without attempting to show how they are different.

The role and status of women in Judaism

Traditionally, Judaism has given different roles to men and women. The role of the man was to be responsible for matters outside the home and to provide what his wife needed to successfully fulfil her role inside the home. Her responsibilities involved caring for their children and bringing them up in a home that reflected their faith. This was seen as a very important role; after all, children are the next generation of adults and parents and they gain their Jewish identity from their mother.

B   *The teacher is using her skills to guide learning*

The woman also had the duty of preparing and baking the challah (a special type of bread), vital for celebration of Shabbat – the most important religious observance that is centred on the home. She lit the candles to welcome Shabbat into the home she managed before her husband broke the bread, said the prayers and passed around the wine. Despite reservations some people have about giving different roles to men and women, these traditional practices still apply. Whether they provide greater status to one of them and, if so, which one, is a matter of debate.

Discussion activity

With a partner, discuss whose role in Shabbat gives them greater status or whether you think the man and woman have equal status. When you have decided, try to think of arguments that support a view you disagree with.

Men have traditionally had distinct roles in the synagogue. For Orthodox Jews, the minyan only counts male Jews and men were expected to play a more active part in worship than women. Nowadays, Orthodox and Reform Jews differ in their practices relating to the role and status of women not only in worship but also in everyday life.

Activities

4   Judaism gives different roles to men and women. Using examples, explain the main difference between their roles.

5   'Judaism is sexist.' Do you agree? Give reasons for your answer showing that you have thought about more than one point of view.

Activities

1   Explain carefully the difference between role and status.

2   Give some examples of roles that carry high status and roles that carry low status. What makes some roles high status and some low status?

3   'Every human being should have the same status regardless of their role.' What do you think of this statement? Explain your opinion.

Summary

You should now know and understand the difference between roles and status and have begun to investigate female roles and status in Judaism.

links

For information on the different roles and status in Jewish worship see pages 120–121.

Orthodox and Reform attitudes towards the role and status of women in Judaism

Orthodox Judaism

The traditional picture of an Orthodox Jewish woman is one of a housekeeper and mother who is expected to take a less active role in society and worship, while her husband works for a living and plays a more active role in society and worship. This is not strictly true today, although some **Orthodox Jews** and especially ultra Orthodox Jews would recognise it. Jewish law does not attempt to regulate every detail in life but provides a structure for a person to express their own personality and spirituality.

The role of wife and mother and the expectation that she will be the home maker existed in most societies throughout the world and did not really change greatly until the 20th century when providing equal opportunities was seen as desirable. However, there are many Orthodox Jews, men and women, who resist these changes, not because they are against equal opportunities, but because they feel their traditional roles offer greater opportunity for spiritual growth. The emphasis on family in the woman's role, nurturing children, and providing opportunities for prayer and celebrating festivals is seen by many to be preferable to the daily chore of working to earn money to enable the role of the home maker to continue. There is nothing in the Torah that prevents women from working for a living or men being responsible for the home and family. It is just that most Orthodox Jews prefer the traditional way.

> It has always been this way so I am happy for it to continue.

> Why would I want to go out to work when looking after my children is much more important?

> I know more than most about my faith and as much as any man does.

 Views of three orthodox Jewish women

Again, it was traditional for women to sit separately from men in the synagogue, watching the worship rather than participating. For men, synagogue attendance was a duty; for a woman, it was something she could do if she wanted. Nowadays, although the separation still exists in some Orthodox synagogues, women are allowed to study the Torah and in some cases to read from it during services. However, they are still very strongly discouraged (but not prevented) from becoming rabbis, possibly due to the attitudes of others in the congregation rather than any scriptural interpretation.

Objectives

Know and understand the difference in attitudes towards women in Orthodox and Reform Judaism.

Express a reasoned opinion about the topic.

Key terms

Orthodox Jews: Jews who believe God gave the complete Torah to Moses and therefore live according to Jewish laws and traditions.

Reform Jews: Jews who believe the Torah was inspired by God and was developed through their history – therefore laws may be changed or adapted as modern life changes.

⊂⊃ links

For a reminder about roles and status, including some roles in Judaism, see 6.1.

AQA Examiner's tip

Remember that not all people think alike. Some Orthodox Jews have 'updated' their thinking more than others. You are likely to be writing about the views of the majority but not every Orthodox or Reform Jew.

Discussion activity

With a partner, discuss the views of the three Orthodox Jewish women. Do you think they sum up accurately the Orthodox view of the role and status of women? Think of a statement a fourth Orthodox Jewish woman might make.

Reform Judaism

The Reform movement grew out of a desire for change in the 19th century. Nowadays **Reform Jews** exist alongside Orthodox Jews despite modernisation brought about by differences in interpretation and a desire to adapt the faith to suit modern conditions. Many Reform Jewish women still choose their traditional roles in the home although some prefer to work for a living, in addition to what they still see as their duty in the home. Many Reform Jewish men make contributions to the home to relieve the pressure and workload on their wives.

Reform synagogues do not promote separation between men and women. Whole families can sit alongside each other and women are allowed to play an active part in worship, including carrying the scrolls when they are paraded from the Ark to the Bimah and reading from them to the congregation. Reform Jewish women are also allowed to become rabbis although male rabbis are still more numerous than female. However, in Britain there are currently twice as many women training to become rabbis than men. The Bat Mitzvah ceremony is also more prominent in Reform synagogues because girls have an equal role in worship to boys.

B *Orthodox Jewish women in Mea Shearim*

Rabbi Jackie Tabick

Rabbi Jackie Tabick became the first female rabbi in Britain. Born in Dublin in 1948, she spent much of her early life in England, completing her rabbi's training at the age of 27. She started her career as the assistant rabbi at the West London Synagogue before moving on to become the rabbi at North West Surrey synagogue in 1998. She is married to a rabbi and they have three children together. Rabbi Tabick has been vice-president of the Movement for Reform Judaism and chair of the World Congress of Faiths. She describes the most rewarding aspect of her work:

'I especially enjoy the teaching and being, I hope, positively engaged in families' lives. I feel honoured that I can sometimes be helpful when people are experiencing great stress.'

www.thejc.com/articles/20083062634/rabbi-jackie-tabick

C *Rabbi Jackie Tabick became Britain's first female rabbi in 1975*

Summary

You should now know and understand different attitudes towards women in Orthodox and Reform Judaism and have expressed reasoned opinions on the topic.

Prejudice

The Jews were the victims of one of the greatest act of **prejudice** that the world has ever seen. In the Second World War, prejudice was the main cause of the deaths of around six million Jewish people in the Holocaust (in Hebrew, the word for the Holocaust is 'shoah', which means 'whirlwind').

Put simply, the word 'prejudice' means to hold an opinion that is not based on any valid reason or evidence. Often it involves a judgement that somebody or something is bad or inferior and this can be a very powerful emotion or feeling. For example, it has been said that Judaism is a sexist religion because it treats women as inferior to men. As you learnt through pages 118–121, the idea that women are treated as inferior to men is not true. They have traditionally had different roles, and in many Jewish families these roles still exist, but their intention was not to give different status to either men or women. They just believed that having different roles was the more natural and the right thing to do and both were highly valued. You may disagree with this but it should not be seen as an example of prejudice, because it didn't lead to the conclusion among Jews that women are inferior to men (or vice versa).

There are several possible reasons why a person may be prejudiced (these are explored in pages 124–125), but whatever the reasons, prejudice can be a destructive way of thinking.

Discrimination

Prejudice becomes a destructive way of thinking when it leads to a person taking action based upon it. If you believe that someone is inferior and of less value to you, there is a chance that you will treat them as such. If, for example, an employer is prejudiced against Jewish people, they may allow their prejudice to deny any Jewish people the opportunity to work for them, even if they are the best applicant for the job. This would be unfair and also illegal under British employment law.

Therefore, **discrimination** can be seen as an action, probably based on prejudice, which leads to unequal and possibly harmful treatment of an individual or group of people. It may be based on race, religion, gender, sexual orientation, age, skin colour etc. but is never based on actual evidence – for example, the individual's qualities and personality – just a wrong and unfair generalisation about the 'category' or group they are seen as coming from.

Some people believe that there is such a thing as positive discrimination. They say that it is perfectly understandable for a Jewish employer to employ a Jewish worker because they have the common bond of their faith. This may mean that there is a greater understanding between the employer and employee and that there would be no problem closing the business early on Friday afternoon in time for the start

Objectives

Understand the meaning of and difference between prejudice and discrimination.

Understand Jewish teachings about prejudice and discrimination.

Key terms

Prejudice: unfairly judging someone before the facts are known.

Discrimination: to act against someone on the basis of sex, race, religion, etc. This is usually a negative action.

⚭ links

For more about the Holocaust, see 6.4, 6.6, 6.9 and 6.10.

Discussion activity

'People being different or having different roles in life only serves to make life more interesting.' Discuss this statement with a partner or in a small group. Do you agree with what it is saying?

A *Prejudice only serves to put barriers between people*

of Shabbat and not expecting them to work on Saturday (Shabbat) for example. While this positive discrimination may be seen to be helpful to the individuals and the business, it may not be seen as helpful to any non-Jews applying to work for the Jewish employer.

Teachings from the Tenakh

There are several references in the Torah that make it quite clear that Jews should not treat people in a way that discriminates against them. They were written at a time when the Hebrews had settled in the Promised Land, despite the fact that there were already non-Hebrews living there.

B *Friendship and tolerance are the enemies of discrimination*

Beliefs and teachings

When an alien (non-Hebrew) lives with you in your land, do not ill-treat him. The alien living with you must be treated as one of your native-born. Love him as yourself for you were aliens in Egypt.

Leviticus 19:33–34

For the Lord your God is God of gods and Lord of lords, the great God, mighty and awesome, who shows no partiality ... he ... loves the alien, giving him food and clothing. And you are to love those who are aliens, for you yourselves were aliens in Egypt.

Deuteronomy 10:17–19

These teachings (and others) make it quite clear that God expects the Jewish people to deal fairly with everybody and treat them as they treat themselves and their families. For Jews, there should be neither prejudice nor discrimination in their dealings with others.

Extension activity

How realistic do you consider these two quotations to be in the 21st century? Give reasons for your answer.

Activities

1   Explain the meaning of both prejudice and discrimination.

2   In a sentence, explain the difference between prejudice and discrimination.

AQA   Examiner's tip

In your exam, don't mix up prejudice and discrimination – prejudice is an attitude or thought, which can lead to discrimination (an action).

Activities

3   Complete this word sum by filling in the blanks (you will need to think about this). There are many correct answers.

'Prejudice + _____ + _____ = discrimination'. Compare your answer with the answers of others.

4   'Positive discrimination is perfectly acceptable.' Do you agree? Give reasons for your answer showing that you have thought about more than one point of view. Refer to Judaism in your answer.

Summary

You should now know and understand the meanings of prejudice and discrimination, the difference between them and some Jewish teaching related to them.

The causes of prejudice and discrimination

Introduction

For many people, identifying why prejudice exists is a difficult task. They may say (quite rightly) that something as illogical and irrational as prejudice cannot possibly have a logical or rational cause. However, it is important to try to discover what causes it because that may help people to find ways of reducing prejudice and its effects.

It may be difficult to appreciate that there may be reasons why some people are prejudiced. Perhaps no number of reasons can justify prejudice, because it is essentially judging something before you have any reason or evidence on which to judge it. Despite this it is important to find out why prejudice exists. Reasons for prejudice that have been put forward include the following:

Fear

Some people feel scared or intimidated by others. If, for example, a woman has been intimidated by a man at some time in her life, it is possible that she will no longer feel comfortable on her own with any man, even one who has no intention of intimidating her or doing her harm.

Victim

It is possible that some people are prejudiced because they themselves have been victims of prejudice. If somebody is attacked by a person with a different skin colour, they may interpret this as being caused by prejudice against them and their experience as a victim may lead them to discriminate against people who have the same skin colour as their attacker.

Ignorance

Some people are ignorant of the beliefs, lifestyle, customs and culture of others. They probably have no understanding of the groups they are prejudiced against. Their lack of information and understanding may prevent them from realising that the ideas on which they base their prejudice are incorrect. They may even be unaware that they have prejudiced attitudes that could lead to discrimination.

Upbringing

The greatest influence on any young person is their home background. If they are brought up surrounded by, for example, racist attitudes, they are more likely to be racist themselves. They may not question these attitudes; they may just accept them as normal and treat people of other races unfairly.

Envy

Poor people may have prejudiced attitudes against rich people out of envy, for example because a rich person has things the poor person doesn't have. Envy can be seen as one reason why Jews may face prejudice (anti-Semitism) because, historically, many Jews have earned large amounts of money by becoming successful business people. However, in running successful businesses, they are helping others by providing opportunities for employment and contributing to the wealth of the nation through trade and taxation.

Objectives

Identify and evaluate what causes prejudice and discrimination.

Discussion activity

Can something as illogical and irrational as prejudice possibly have a logical or rational cause? Spend two minutes discussing this question in a small group. Be prepared to share your ideas.

Activities

1 Copy the diagram (below). Around the outside put the seven causes of prejudice as mentioned on these pages. For each write no more than ten words of explanation and draw a neat symbol for each one.

— Causes of prejudice —

2 Can you think of any more causes of prejudice? You can add them to your spidergram if you wish.

Scapegoating

Certain minority groups of people are unfairly blamed for causing problems that have nothing to do with them. Others are encouraged to believe that it is the minority group's fault and are prejudiced against them. Before and during the Second World War, Hitler's government in Germany unfairly and incorrectly blamed the Jews for the economic and social problems Germany faced and therefore discriminated against them. They (along with some other minority groups) became scapegoats. This is one of the reasons why the Holocaust was allowed to happen without mass protests from ordinary Germans (some of whom knew it was happening but perhaps not on such a massive scale).

Stereotyping

This is the idea that everybody in a group is the same. There are people in any group who don't do the right thing all the time but that does not mean that all members of the group are like that and therefore should be treated unfairly. Again, this was a factor that contributed to the Holocaust.

These seven causes can all contribute to prejudice, which itself leads to discrimination.

Activity

5   For each of the two people below, write ten words that you think describe each of them.

A

How did you choose your ten words that describe each person (right)? You were only able to base your judgements on their appearance because you cannot possibly know anything more about either of them. Your descriptions are possibly quite negative; they might be quite correct but they might represent a complete misjudgement.

Both these people could be intending to train to be surgeons having spent two years nursing their mothers and preparing them for death due to a terminal illness. Making judgements based on a person's appearance, for example, can be very dangerous, because such judgements could lead to prejudice and discrimination.

∞ links

For more about the origins of scapegoating, see 3.5 pages 60–61 about Yom Kippur.

Activities

3   Which of the causes of prejudice do you think is the most difficult to overcome? Give your reasons.

4   'It is good to have a scapegoat because you can blame everything on it and not feel guilty.' What do you think? Explain your opinion.

Extension activity

Do you think any of these causes make you sympathetic towards those who are prejudiced? Give clear reasons for your answer.

Summary

You should now be able to identify and evaluate some of the main causes of prejudice and discrimination.

Prejudice and discrimination against Jews

History

Judaism is strongly associated with Israel, even though today more Jewish people live around the globe than in Israel. Israel is the Jewish homeland, the land Jews believe that God promised them and helped them to conquer at the time of the Exodus. In 1948, the state of Israel was established as an independent state by the United Nations as part of the settlement at the end of the Second World War. However, since 1948, Israel has been involved in several conflicts with its neighbours and there have been many arguments about defending territory and security, relating both to Israel and to the countries that border it. In 2008–9, there was conflict between the Israeli army and Palestinians in Gaza. Whatever the rights and wrongs of the conflict, opposition to Israel in the international community grew as a result.

Unfortunately, as Israel is so strongly identified with Judaism, even though Israel has a secular government, some saw it as a conflict between the Jews from Israel and the Muslims living in Gaza. The conflict may have been political, but many saw this as a religious conflict. Consequently prejudice against Judaism (sometimes called antisemitism) grew as people protested against Israel's involvement in Gaza because they could not separate national and political considerations from religious ones.

Objectives

Consider prejudice against Jewish people.

Investigate the effects of prejudice on Jewish people.

A Israel and neighbours

Activities

1. Explain why some people saw the conflict in Gaza as a religious one rather than a political one.
2. Why did the conflict in Gaza provoke antisemitism in some people?

Prejudice against Jews in Britain

Prejudice against Jews has existed in Britain for many years. In 2008, there were around 550 reported incidents of such prejudice in Britain but in the first few weeks of 2009, the ongoing war in Gaza resulted in a rise to seven a day of reported attacks against Jews, including graffiti, hate emails and physical violence. Police in Jewish areas were put on high alert and were instructed to be vigilant, looking out for possible incidents of prejudice against Jews.

The effect of this prejudice is that some Jewish families decided to emigrate to countries such as the USA where they felt they could live in greater safety than in Britain. For others, it made them more vigilant and restricted the activities that they would normally be involved in, including not allowing their children to spend time involved in community activities in the synagogue unless they were accompanied by an adult. The Parliamentary Committee against Antisemitism investigated this situation and recommended ways of tackling it.

Activities

3. In which year did Israel become an independent state?
4. Explain why it is difficult to separate racial and religious prejudice against Jews.

Mark Frazer, spokesman for the Board of Deputies of British Jews, said:

> We are seeing an unprecedented level of attacks directed at the Jewish community, both physical and verbal.

© Copyright Guardian News & Media Ltd 2009

▊ The Jewish Council for Racial Equality (JCORE)

In 1976, JCORE was established to try to combat discrimination and promote racial justice in Britain. They work to establish social justice and challenge the existence of racism at its roots by working closely with other minority ethnic communities and refugee organisations, with anti-racist organisations, interfaith groups, schools, colleges, community and youth groups, and other agencies promoting racial and religious equality.

B *Jewish sixth-formers delivering Hanukkah cards to Downing Street in support of refugees in the Darfur region of Sudan during a time of conflict, fuelled by prejudice, that has seen thousands of civilians killed*

They offer a wide range of resources and information sheets to highlight current social justice issues, which can be used by school and community groups and have an education team to prepare and deliver programmes aimed at eliminating prejudice by teaching people about the background and effects of it.

One of their supporters, Rabbi Hugo Gryn, summed up the need for groups like JCORE:

> 66 *I always think that the real offenders at the half-way mark of the last century were the bystanders – all those people who let things happen because it didn't affect them directly.* 99

www.jcore.org.uk

Summary

You should now know about prejudice against Jews, understand how it affects Jewish people and have studied some Jewish responses to it.

Research activity

Look at www.bod.org.uk to find out about the Board of Deputies of British Jews and the stance they take on topical issues.

JCORE
JEWISH COUNCIL
FOR RACIAL EQUALITY

C

Activities

5   Write a letter to a person who has shown prejudice towards Jews expressing your feelings about their actions and explaining why it is a wrong thing to do.

6   Explain how JCORE is trying to help reduce prejudice and discrimination.

Discussion activity

With a partner, discuss how you feel about Rabbi Hugo Gryn's statement. Is he correct or is he being unfair to those who let dreadful things happen? Be prepared to share your opinion and reasons with others.

Extension activity

Do you think there is any way of stopping prejudice against Jews? Give reasons for your answer.

Definition

Persecution is when a person or group is systematically ill treated, possibly as a result of prejudice. This may be done by a government, group of people or an individual. Bullying can be seen as a form of persecution.

Persecution in ancient times

The Tenakh gives many accounts of persecution, conquest and defeat, primarily in the Books of Kings. These two books start with King David in around 1000 BCE and finish with the Babylonian conquest of Jerusalem in 597 BCE. Throughout this time, the political and religious differences between the Jews and their neighbours provoked conflict as one empire after another (e.g. Assyrians, Babylonians) swallowed up the small area of land on which the Jews had established themselves, invading, occupying and ruling it without the consent of the Jews.

As with other nations that were conquered, the conquerors used persecution to try to force the Jews to adopt their culture and religion. However, it soon became clear to them that the Jewish religion, based on one God and including a strong ethical structure, was more advanced than any other belief system they had met. Often, therefore, the conquerors accepted that the Jews were so determined to keep their faith alive that it was easier to allow them to do so.

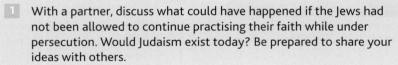

Discussion activity

1   With a partner, discuss what could have happened if the Jews had not been allowed to continue practising their faith while under persecution. Would Judaism exist today? Be prepared to share your ideas with others.

However, this didn't prevent the Babylonians from taking the influential Jews into exile elsewhere in their empire, in the hope that the people who were left would be easier to control without influential leadership. This exile is famously recorded in Psalm 137.

Beliefs and teachings

By the rivers of Babylon we sat and wept when we remembered Zion (Jerusalem).

There on the poplars we hung our harps,

for there our captors asked us for songs ...

they said, 'Sing us one of the songs of Zion!'

How can we sing the songs of the Lord while in a foreign land?

Psalm 137:1–4

Objectives

Trace the persecution of the Jewish people at various points in their history.

Analyse how persecution has affected Jewish life through the centuries.

Key terms

Persecution: oppression or maltreatment of people because of their beliefs, race or religion.

Discussion activity

2   Discuss with a partner whether if persecution was a way of life for many in ancient times, we should just accept that it happened and forget about it.

A   *The Assyrians captured Israel in 721 BCE and deported many Jews to neighbouring countries*

Persecution during the Second World War

The worst period of persecution in Jewish history was during the Second World War when more than a quarter of the world's Jewish population – around six million people – were murdered in concentration camps and death camps in Europe.

This was the worst and final act of the persecution of European Jews under Hitler's regime in Germany which had begun before the start of the Second World War. Hitler came to power in 1933 and in the same year he ruled that Jews were banned from working in the civil service, legal professions, schools, universities or in publishing newspapers. By 1935, they were no longer considered to be citizens of Germany.

On 9 November 1938, Hitler ordered military forces to attack Jews, their businesses and synagogues. That night 91 Jews were killed, hundreds were injured, 7,500 Jewish stores were looted and 177 synagogues were burned down and destroyed. This became known as Kristallnacht – the Night of Broken Glass. In the same year a few hundred thousand Jews were allowed to leave Germany after surrendering all their assets (homes, businesses and possessions) to Hitler's government. Remaining Jews were forced to wear a yellow Star of David as a means of identification and mockery.

B *A synagogue burns in Ober Ramstadt, 9 November 1938*

⬤⬤ links

For more on concentration camps and death camps see 6.9 and 6.10, pages 134–137.

Summary

You should now know about persecution and how it has affected Jews at various times in their history.

Attitudes to suffering (1)

Introduction

The fact that people suffer leads some people to doubt God's existence. They ask how a loving and just God can allow good people to suffer. Some people use this as evidence against God's existence, believing that if he existed, he wouldn't allow the suffering. At times in their history, most notably during the Holocaust, this question has concerned millions of Jews. However, many Jews saw their faith as a source of strength to overcome their suffering, rather than giving in to persecution and losing their faith.

Origins of suffering

In order to find the origins of suffering, Jews look right back to the time of Adam and Eve and their disobedience in eating the forbidden fruit in the Garden of Eden. In the story in Genesis, God told them that the result of their disobedience was that they would face suffering throughout their lives. God said to Eve:

> **Beliefs and teachings**
>
> I will greatly increase your pains in childbearing; with pain you will give birth to children.
>
> *Genesis* 3:16

whereas Adam's punishment would be felt by all people:

> **Beliefs and teachings**
>
> Cursed is the ground because of you; through painful toil you will eat of it all the days of your life.
>
> It will produce thorns and thistles for you, and you will eat the plants of the field.
>
> *Genesis* 3:17–18

While not all Jews take this story as literal truth, they do use it to explain why suffering exists. It exists not because of God but because of people's disobedience to his instructions. However, suffering cannot be interpreted as God punishing individuals who disobey him because some of the worst people the world has seen have not suffered greatly, while some of the most godly people who have ever lived have had to endure great suffering.

Objectives

Investigate the origins and causes of suffering.

Understand two stories from the Tenakh.

Discussion activity

Spend three minutes with a partner discussing whether the existence of suffering means there is no God. If there is a God, why does he allow suffering?

Research activity

Look at the whole story of Adam and Eve's disobedience in Genesis 3:1–24.

Who do you think is to blame: the serpent for tempting Eve; Eve for giving into temptation and offering the fruit to Adam; or Adam for taking the fruit from Eve? Why do you think this?

A *Adam and Eve are banished from the Garden of Eden*

The story of Job

The book of Job in the Ketuvim is a biography of a man called Job (pronounced "Jobe"). It is included in the Tenakh because it attempts to use the example of one man to explain about suffering. Again, it is probably not intended to be taken literally but it teaches important lessons about suffering. This is a simple retelling of the story:

Case study

The story of Job

Job was a prosperous God-fearing man who had seven sons and three daughters. The angels of Heaven together with Satan met with God and God asked Satan for his opinion about Job. Satan agreed he was a pious (highly religious) man but that this was as a result of his prosperity and wealth. If he was poor, Satan thought he would not be so pious. In response, and to test Satan's statement about Job, God gave Satan permission to slowly destroy Job's possessions and children. Satan duly obliged and eventually Job fell to the ground and said to God:

'Naked I came from my mother's womb, and naked I shall depart.

The Lord gave and the Lord has taken away; may the name of the Lord be praised' (Job 1:21)

Satan then asked for and was granted permission to cause physical harm to Job but in a way that didn't threaten his life. He afflicted him with dreadful boils and despite prompting from his wife to curse God, Job refused to do so.

Four friends visited Job in his misfortune and in long speeches, three of them tried to get him to confess his sins to God, because they thought God would only punish a sinner in this way and therefore Job must have sinned a great deal. Job refused because he believed he was without sin. Eventually, God spoke to Job, giving him a poetic picture of his power and wisdom and pointing out to him that God has absolute freedom over his creation. He made it clear that Job's inability to see the world as God does was the reason for him misunderstanding God's reasons for allowing him to suffer.

In the end, Job was restored to health, given twice as much wealth as he had previously, seven more sons and three more daughters, and was allowed to live for a further 140 years before dying peacefully of old age.

B   *An engraving of Job and his friends by Gustave Doré*

AQA   Examiner's tip

Although you will not be asked to write down this story in your examination, you can use it as an example of a Jew who has suffered if you wish.

Summary

You should now have considered two stories from the Tenakh to help you understand Jewish beliefs about the origins and reasons for suffering.

Vicarious suffering

Vicarious suffering is one of the easier types of suffering to explain. It means to suffer on behalf of somebody else and can be seen as an admirable thing to do. The book of Isaiah has a vivid picture of vicarious suffering, the meaning of which Jewish scholars have debated and considered for centuries.

Beliefs and teachings

Surely he took up our infirmities and carried our sorrows, yet we considered him stricken by God, smitten by him and afflicted …
He was oppressed and afflicted, yet he did not open his mouth; he was led like a lamb to the slaughter, and as a sheep before her slaughterers is silent, so he did not open his mouth …
He was assigned a grave with the wicked, and with the rich in his death, though he had done no violence, nor was any deceit in his mouth. Therefore I will give him a portion among the great, and he will divide the spoils with the strong, because he poured out his life unto death.

Isaiah 53:4–12

Whether this unidentified man was a real person in the past, present or future or the product of the writer's imagination or inspiration, invented to make a point, is not known but it does show a belief in suffering on behalf of someone else as something credit-worthy.

Activities

1. Explain what vicarious suffering is.
2. Can you think of any examples of vicarious suffering?

Research activity

Read the whole passage in Isaiah 53:1–12. Jot down your thoughts about this passage.

Other Jewish attitudes to suffering

Many Jews believe that suffering has a positive side to it. The rabbis responsible for the Talmud explained that suffering:

- is a way of cleansing people from sin
- encourages people to reflect on what they have done wrong
- helps people to realise the need for repentance to bring them back to God
- is a way of God testing the righteous
- may be a result of the 'sins' of the generation and not the individual.

However, Jews have a responsibility to help to relieve suffering. Various relief organisations such as World Jewish Relief have been set up to do this worldwide and individuals have a duty to offer money or practical help where there is a need. Even children are encouraged to get

Objectives

Know and understand some more Jewish attitudes to suffering.

Analyse the link between suffering and justice.

AQA Examiner's tip

You will not be expected to know such a long quotation but it will help to have studied how Jews have considered suffering.

A   *Sculpture of the prophet Isaiah*

Activities

3. Think carefully about the Talmudic explanations for suffering. Which do you think provides the best explanation for the existence of suffering?
4. Now put the other four explanations into your own order from second best to worst. Explain the reasons for your most and least important explanation.

involved through the use of a pushke in which they put coins, which are then given to the needy.

However, these attitudes do not mean that Jews just accept suffering if there is something they can do about it. Justice is one of the cornerstones of Judaism so anybody causing others to suffer should be brought to justice. Justice is seen as best when tempered with mercy (compassion), but this does not mean that those who cause suffering should be allowed to get away with it – justice is supported and maintained by fair punishment.

Discussion activity

Discuss with a partner or in a small group whether you think that those brought to justice for causing suffering to others should be shown mercy. If so, what kind of mercy?

B *Simon Wiesenthal – promoter of justice and avenger of evil*

Case study

Simon Wiesenthal

Simon Wiesenthal was a Ukrainian Jew who was born in 1908. Between 1941 and 1945, he was imprisoned in various forced labour camps and concentration camps including Auschwitz and Buchenwald. He escaped from a work camp in 1943 but was recaptured a few months later. When peace was declared in 1945 and the concentration camps were liberated he was close to death but medical care ensured that he managed to survive. He was reunited with his wife who escaped the Holocaust by taking a non-Jewish identity, but they learnt that 89 of their relatives had died.

The rest of his life was dedicated to hunting down Nazi war criminals and bringing them to justice. He established the Simon Wiesenthal Centre, whose mission was to identify and help capture those who had played a part in the Holocaust. Their greatest success came in 1959 when they tracked down Adolf Eichmann, the mastermind behind the policy of exterminating European Jews. In 1961, Eichmann was found guilty and executed. Simon Wiesenthal expressed sadness at the execution because he thought justice would have been better served by keeping him alive.

Simon Wiesenthal's life was dominated by suffering both during the war and after it. Rather than trying to live a normal life and blocking out his horrific experiences, he remained dedicated to reliving the Holocaust in the cause of ensuring that those who caused the suffering were brought to justice. He famously said:

> 'For me the Holocaust was not only a Jewish tragedy but also a human tragedy. After the war, when I saw that the Jews were talking only about the tragedy of six million Jews, I sent letters to Jewish organisations asking them to talk also about the millions of others who were persecuted with us together – many of them only because they helped Jews.'

> *en.thinkexist.com*

Awarded an honorary knighthood from the Queen in 2004, Simon Wiesenthal died in 2005 aged 96. The Simon Wiesenthal Centre lives on to promote justice throughout the world and fight prejudice against Jewish people wherever it occurs.

Activities

5 Write an outline account of the suffering experienced by Simon Wiesenthal.

6 Do you think justice was served when Adolf Eichmann was executed? Explain why.

7 Do you agree with Simon Wiesenthal's quotation about the Holocaust being a human tragedy, not just a Jewish one? Give your reasons.

8 'Simon Wiesenthal should have lived a normal life after the war instead of reliving his suffering daily.' What do you think? Explain your opinion.

Extension activity

Using the internet, read more about the life of Simon Wiesenthal. Do you think he deserved to be awarded an honorary knighthood by the Queen? Explain your reasons.

Summary

You should now know and understand more about Jewish attitudes to suffering and be able to link suffering to justice.

6.9   The Holocaust – background and effects

Background to the Holocaust

In 1918, the treaty of Versailles settled the outstanding issues from the First World War. As a result of this treaty, Germany lost about 12 per cent of its territory, most of the German coal and steel industry and had to disband its army. The Germans were also forced to pay huge sums of money for the damage the war had caused to countries they were fighting against. As a result of this, the German economy was unable to grow, unemployment rose and extremist political parties offered solutions that seemed attractive to a struggling population. One such party was the National Socialist (Nazi) party led by Adolf Hitler, which was elected to power in 1933.

They had two objectives:

- to build up the army, produce weapons and use them to restore the greatness of Germany;
- to provide innocent targets that the German people could direct their anger towards, blaming them for the country's problems (scapegoating).

The largest group of people who became targets were the Jews. They were accused of controlling the banks and the supply of money, having too much influence on the professional classes and in the universities, and being in league with the communists. In other words, Germany's problems were seen to be the fault of the Jews. These unjust accusations were levelled at the Jews with such force and intensity that the German people had little option but to believe them.

So what happened next?

By the start of the Second World War in 1939, the persecution against the Jews was hitting them hard. They had no rights of citizenship in Germany and their normal way of life was greatly affected. Many could not work, their businesses had been closed or taken over and their movements were heavily restricted. Once the Second World War started, things became even worse. In countries in which the Nazis took control, they imposed similar restrictions on the Jews before, in many towns and cities, ordering them to leave their homes, taking what few possessions they could carry, to live in ghettoes – poor parts of cities, controlled by the Nazis. These became massively overcrowded with many families living in each small house. The overcrowding situation was eased by transporting thousands to concentration camps, where some were put to work while the majority were murdered. On 20 January 1942, The 'Final Solution to the Jewish Question', the product of a meeting between 15 high-ranking Nazi party and government leaders, formalised this as policy at a meeting at Wannsee in Berlin. By the end of the Second World War, around six million Jews from countries as far apart as Norway, France, Russia and Greece were killed. In Poland, the number killed (three million) amounted to 90 per cent of the country's Jewish population.

Objectives

Understand the causes and development of the Holocaust.

Use a case study to show the way the Holocaust affected the Jewish people.

links

Look back at pages 60–61 for more about the origins of scapegoats.

Key terms

Holocaust: (Hebrew – Shoah) the murder of six million Jews during the Second World War.

Discussion activity

Discuss the following statement with a small group: 'If the First World War hadn't happened, nor would the Second World War have happened, and if the Second World War hadn't happened, the Holocaust wouldn't have happened.'

Activity

1   Explain in detail how making the Jews scapegoats helped to justify the Holocaust to the German people.

links

See 6.6 on page 128 for the beginnings of the persecution that led to the Holocaust.

לזכר עולם משפחת פרבר
Thou Shall Not Kill
In Loving Memory of the
FERBER FAMILY
88 Members Murdered by the Nazi's
Holocaust 1939 - 1945
May their Souls be Eternally Blessed
Dedicated by the Survivors
Fred Ferber   Roman Ferber

A *Plaque outside Remuh synagogue, Krakow, Poland*

The Eagle Pharmacy, Krakow, Poland

The ghetto in Krakow was established in March 1941 in the district of Podgorze. It consisted of 15 streets and 320 houses, most of which were quite small, and a square where inhabitants had to assemble if the Nazi 'guards' required them to. It was surrounded by a barbed wire fence and later a wall with four gates, all guarded by armed Nazi soldiers. Population numbers fluctuated but, at its height, the ghetto housed 15,000 people. As Jews died or were transported to concentration camps, other Jews took their place. Disease was a major problem that killed thousands.

Tadeusz Pankiewicz, a non-Jew, owned the Eagle Pharmacy on the edge of the square. He refused orders to leave the ghetto and stayed there throughout the war, providing vital medical services to the inhabitants of the ghetto. His staff left the ghetto at the end of each working day but he remained there in case an emergency arose in the night. The pharmacy became a meeting place and shelter where people could meet up with others and try to forget the situation they faced for a short time. The staff tried to update the population with news and secretly delivered food and money into the ghetto. At times of deportations to concentration camps, the pharmacy became a place of farewell and valuable possessions including Torah scrolls were hidden there. They also hid people so the Nazis could not find and kill them. In each of these actions, Tadeusz and his staff risked their own lives on a daily basis.

Tadeusz Pankiewicz survived the war and worked in the Eagle Pharmacy until 1953 and then at another pharmacy in Krakow until 1974. He was called to give evidence at trials of several Nazi war criminals and in 1983 was honoured by the government of Israel as a non-Jew who saved Jewish lives. He died in 1993.

B   *A remaining part of the Krakow ghetto wall. What does the shape remind you of?*

Activities

4   Write a couple of paragraphs as a Jew in the Krakow ghetto who used the Eagle Pharmacy. What were your living conditions like? Did anyone become ill and die? What use did you make of the Eagle Pharmacy? Were you able to keep your faith or did you feel like giving it up? What did you expect would happen to you?

5   'We haven't learnt the lesson of the Holocaust because prejudice still exists.' Write your thoughts about this statement. You may want to briefly discuss it with a partner first.

Summary

You should now understand the causes and development of the Holocaust and how it affected Jewish people in Europe.

Auschwitz – a background

In 1940, as part of the Nazi 'final solution', a former Polish army barracks at Oswiecim was established as the Auschwitz I concentration camp. It was to be used for Jews and other minority groups such as gypsies and homosexuals whom the Nazis did not wish to include in the type of society that they wanted to create. People were forced to travel from all over Europe, usually by train, to work or to meet their death here. Soon after, in 1942, two more concentration camps opened close by at Birkenau (Auschwitz II) and a small one at Monowice (Auschwitz III).

The intention of those in charge of the camps was to force prisoners to work. The words above the gate of Auschwitz I 'Arbeit macht frei' literally means 'Work will set you free'. Those who could not work (children, the elderly, the disabled and women) were killed. From late 1941, those who were to be killed were told that they were going to shower but instead of water, deadly Zyklon B gas was released inside the communal shower room. Their bodies were cremated in the attached crematoria and their possessions, including spectacles, shoes and personal effects were sent to a storage building called Canada where they were sorted out for re-use. The hair was removed from the dead bodies to be used for weaving into cloth used in the creation of uniforms for the enforced labourers.

Those who could work were housed in appalling conditions. Many of them did not survive for more than a few months before they died or were killed because they were no longer of any use. Troublemakers received severe physical punishments such as starvation in Auschwitz I block 11 alongside 'the wall of death' – the place where other troublemakers were taken to be shot after having been stripped naked. Some others, especially twins, were used in medical experimentation under the command of Dr Joseph Mengele.

Objectives

Use a case study to understand the experience of a concentration camp.

Understand something of the life of those who lived and died in concentration camps.

Activities

1　Explain how Auschwitz I was used during the Second World War.

2　How did the Nazis justify choosing people such as Jews, gypsies and homosexuals to be placed in concentration camps?

3　Look carefully at the photos in Source A. They were taken in 2008 at Auschwitz I and Auschwitz II. What are your thoughts as you consider these pictures?

4　Do you think these two camps should have been completely destroyed once the war was over?

A Auschwitz

Auschwitz II – Birkenau

Two kilometres to the west of Auschwitz I stands Auschwitz II – Birkenau. This is a vast site with a railway line running down the middle of it. Much of it was destroyed just before it was liberated but enough of it remains to convey the true horror of what happened there. Prisoners were brought straight into the camp in crowded trains. Some who travelled long distances did not survive the journey because the carriages were so cramped, hot and lacking in air. Exit from the trains was strictly, and in some instances violently, controlled and as the prisoners stepped onto the platform that had been built specially for the purpose, they were briefly inspected by doctors who decided their fate.

Men and women were separated and if they were able to work, they were housed in long sheds, on either side of the railway line side. Those who couldn't work were often immediately led to one of the gas chambers at the far end of the camp and killed.

The camps were liberated early in 1945 and the true horror of what had been happening there was exposed to the rest of the world. It is estimated that between one-and-a-half million and two million people died in the three Auschwitz camps, the large majority of them Jews.

Case study

Anne Frank

Anne Frank was born in June 1929 to a Jewish family living in Holland. She kept a diary between June 1942 and August 1944 outlining her thoughts and experiences as a young Jewish girl in a Nazi occupied country during the Second World War. Despite the desperate times, along with the majority of Jews, she kept her faith in God and found that it gave her strength. From July 1942, she and her family were forced to live in hiding from the Nazis. In August 1944 their whereabouts were discovered and the family was transported to Auschwitz. A few weeks later Anne and her elder sister Margot were relocated to Belsen concentration camp where they both died from typhus in March 1945, just a few weeks before the camp was liberated by British troops. Her writings were first published in 1947 and have become an inspiration to millions of readers ever since. The following extract shows her hope for a better future and the strength of her faith in God despite what was happening.

'Who has inflicted this upon us? Who has made us Jews different from all other people? Who has allowed us to suffer so terribly up till now? It is God that has made us as we are, but it will be God, too, who will raise us up again. If we bear all this suffering and if there are still Jews left, when it is over, then Jews, instead of being doomed, will be held up as an example.'

Anne Frank, Diary of a Young Girl (1947), entry dated 11 April 1944

Activities

5   Why was Auschwitz II needed?

6   Explain how Auschwitz II was used during the Second World War.

Extension activity

1   All prisoners at Auschwitz were branded with a number before being put to work. Why do you think the Nazi's did this? What effect do you think it had on the prisoner?

Extension activity

2   How do you think Anne Frank's life was influenced by her faith in God? What do you think the quotation from 11 April 1944 tells us about Anne's faith?

Research activity

Try to obtain and read a copy of Anne Frank's *Diary of a Young Girl*. Alternatively, her life story was dramatised as *The Diary of Anne Frank* in 2008 by the BBC and is available on DVD.

Discussion activity

With a partner, discuss your feelings about what you have just learnt.

AQA   Examiner's tip

You can use Anne Frank as an example of a Jew who never lost her faith in God despite her wartime experiences and tragic death.

Summary

You should now know about and understand the experience prisoners in concentration camps faced and, using the example of Anne Frank, how their faith gave them strength and hope.

Justice and equality – summary

For the examination, you should now be able to:

✔ show understanding of Jewish ideas on prejudice, discrimination, women and suffering in:

- the role and status of women
- different approaches to the role and status of women in Orthodox and Reform Judaism
- prejudice and discrimination, with reference to race and religion
- the Jewish experience of persecution
- Jewish attitudes to suffering
- the Holocaust

✔ apply relevant Jewish teachings to each topic

✔ discuss topics from different points of view, including Jewish ones.

Sample answer

1 Write an answer to the following exam question.

'Religious prejudice is not as bad as racism.'

What do you think? Explain your opinion. *(3 marks)*

2 Read the following sample answer:

> I think racism is worse than religious prejudice because a person has no choice about their race but can choose their religion. Both are bad but racism is worse.

3 With a partner, discuss the sample answer. Do you think that there are other things that the student could have included in the answer?

4 What mark would you give this answer out of six? Look at the mark scheme in the Introduction on page 7 (AO2). What are the reasons for the mark you have given?

AQA Examination-style questions

1 Look at the photograph below and answer the following questions.

(a) Explain the difference between the views of Orthodox and Reform Jews on the role of women.

(6 marks)

As there are six marks available for this question you should try to spend about seven minutes thinking about and writing your answer.

(b) Explain, giving examples, the meaning of the word prejudice.

(4 marks)

As you are asked to give examples, you cannot gain full marks without any.

(c) 'It is best for men and women to worship separately.' Do you agree? Give reasons for your answer showing that you have thought about more than one point of view. Refer to Judaism in your answer.

(6 marks)

Try to think why you hold your opinion and reasons why people may hold a different opinion from you. Write them in separate paragraphs and don't forget to include some Jewish teachings.

Glossary

A

Amidah: the standing prayer, said standing at all services.

Aron Hakodesh: the Ark – part of the synagogue containing Torah scrolls.

B

Bar Mitzvah: celebration of a boy coming of age at 13. Literally 'son of commandment'.

Bat Chayil: celebration of a girl coming of age at 12, in Orthodox Synagogues. Literally 'daughter of valour'.

Bat Mitzvah: celebration of a girl coming of age at 12, in Reform Synagogues. Literally 'daughter of the commandment'.

Bet Din: religious court, made up of rabbis.

Betrothal: an engagement, traditionally 12 months before a Jewish wedding.

Bimah: a platform in a synagogue from which the Torah is read.

Brit Milah: circumcision; the removal of the foreskin for religious reasons.

C

Chametz (Leaven): leavened foods, prohibited during the festival of Pesach (Passover).

Chazzan (cantor): a person who leads or chants prayers in the synagogue.

Chuppah: the canopy traditionally used at Jewish weddings.

Circumcision: the removal of the foreskin from the penis.

D

Discrimination: to act against someone on the basis of sex, race, religion, etc. This is usually a negative action.

Divorce: legal ending of a marriage.

E

equality: that people should be given the same rights and opportunities regardless of sex, religion, race, etc.

F

Festival: a religious celebration or commemoration.

G

Gemara: a commentary on the Mishnah which is part of the Talmud.

H

Haggadah: text read during the Passover seder recounting the story of the Exodus.

Halakhah: the code of conduct for Jewish life.

Holocaust: (Hebrew – Shoah) the murder of six million Jews during the Second World War.

I

Israel: 1 The ancient name for the Jewish people;
2 The modern Jewish country in the Middle East;
3 Literally means "One who struggles with God".

J

Justice: bringing about what is right, fair and according to the law or making up for a wrong that has been committed.

K

Kaddish: An important and central prayer in the Jewish prayer service.

Kittel: a white Jewish robe worn on solemn occasions and often used as a burial shroud.

Ketuvim: the third section of the Tenakh – the writings.

Kippah: a skull cap.

Kosher: food that meets Jewish laws.

M

Marriage: a legal union between a man and a woman.

Matzah (plural matzoh): the unleavened bread eaten at Passover (Pesach).

Menorah: a seven-branched candlestick.

Messianic Age: when God's anointed one will come and lead the Jews.

Mezuzah: a scroll, containing the Shema.

Minyan: a quorum of ten men required for a service.

Mishnah: The first written version of the oral tradition; the authoritative document was put together in 200 C.E.

Mitzvot: Jewish rules or commandments.

Mohel: a man trained to carry out Jewish circumcisions.

Mourning: a period of time spent remembering a person who has died.

N

Ner Tamid: a light kept burning in the synagogue – continual light.

Nevi'im: The second section of the Tenakh – the prophets.

O

Orthodox Jews: Jews who believe God gave the complete Torah to Moses and therefore live according to Jewish laws and traditions.

P

Persecution: oppression or maltreatment of people because of their beliefs, race or religion.

Pesach (Passover): festival in remembrance of the Jewish Exodus from Egypt. Celebrated in spring.

Pilgrimage: a journey to a holy site. Pilgrimage is itself an act of worship and devotion.

Prejudice: unfairly judging someone before the facts are known.

R

Rabbi: a religious leader and teacher.

Redeemer: one who redeems and saves from the consequences of sin.

Reform Jews: Jews who believe the Torah was inspired by God and was developed through their history – therefore laws may be changed or adapted as modern life changes.

Responsa: The correspondence of Rabbis concerning religious decisions.

Role: the actions a person performs; what they do.

Rosh Hashanah: the Jewish New Year.

S

Seder: the ceremonial dinner on the first night (or both nights) of Passover (Pesach).

Shabbat: holy day of the week; day of spiritual renewal beginning at sunset on Friday and continuing to nightfall on Saturday.

Shema: Jewish prayer affirming belief in the one God, found in the Torah.

Shofar: a ram's horn, which is blown like a trumpet particularly during Rosh Hashanah and Yom Kippur.

Siddur: 'order': prayer book for daily, Sabbath and occasional use.

Star of David: A symbol of Judaism said to represent the shield of King David who ruled Israel in the 10th century BCE (Magen David).

Status: how important a person's role makes them in other people's estimation.

Synagogue: building for Jewish public prayer, study and gathering.

T

Tallit: a prayer shawl.

Talmud: Commentary by the rabbis on the Torah – Mishnah and Gemara together in one collection.

Tashlich: performed on the afternoon of Rosh Hashanah (the Jewish New Year). The previous year's sins are symbolically "cast off" by throwing pieces of bread, or a similar food item, into flowing water, e.g. a river.

Tefillin: small leather boxes containing extracts from the Torah, strapped to the believer's arms and forehead for morning prayers.

Tenakh (Tanakh): The 24 books of the Jewish Bible.

The Covenant: God's agreement to look after the Jews as his chosen people, subject to Israel's obedience.

Torah: 1 The five books of Moses and first section of the Tenakh – the law;
2 The whole of Jewish teaching.

Trefah: forbidden food – means 'torn'.

W

Western Wall: The only part of the ancient Temple of Herod remaining – Jews come to pray there – a place of pilgrimage.

Worship: a specific act of religious devotion.

Y

Yad Vashem: a memorial to the Holocaust victims in Jerusalem – means 'a memorial and a name'.

Yahrzeit candle: candle lit on the annual anniversary of a death.

Yamulkah: another name for the kippah, the skull cap worn during prayers and Torah study. Some Orthodox men wear it continually.

Yeshiva: A college where the Torah and Talmud are studied.

Yom Kippur: the Day of Atonement – a day of fasting on the tenth day after Rosh Hashanah.

Index